THE POLITICAL PAINTINGS OF MERLYN EVANS

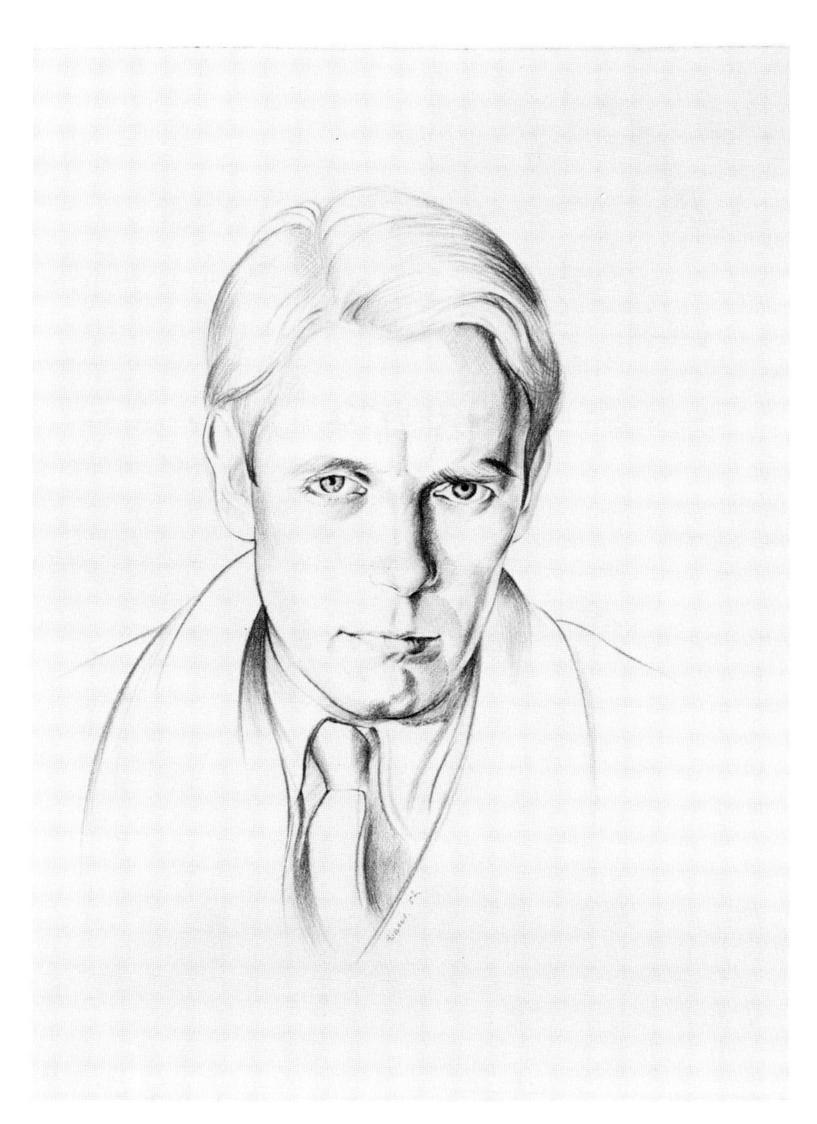

THE POLITICAL PAINTINGS OF
MERLYN EVANS

—— 1930-1950 ——

THE TATE GALLERY

cover
Merlyn Evans
The Conflict (No.1)
August–October 1940
(cat.no.17)

frontispiece
Merlyn Evans
Self Portrait 1952
(cat.no.32)

ISBN 0 946590 22 2
Published by order of the Trustees 1985
for the exhibition of 27 March–2 June 1985
Copyright © 1985 The Tate Gallery All rights reserved
Published by Tate Gallery Publications, Millbank,
London SW1P 4RG Designed by Caroline Johnston
Colour photography by John Webb Printed in Great Britain
by Balding + Mansell Limited, Wisbech, Cambs

Contents

7   **Preface**   *Alan Bowness*

8   **Acknowledgements**

9   **Introduction**   *David Fraser Jenkins*

17   **Merlyn Evans's Use of Egg Tempera**   *Tim Green*

20   **Background**   *Merlyn Evans, 1956*

29   **Catalogue**

44   **Biography to 1950**

46   **Selected Exhibitions**

47   **List of Lenders**

Preface

Merlyn Evans was something of an outsider in British art, perhaps even a lost leader, born out of his time. I have always felt that his remarkable gifts as an artist would have come to a happier fruition had he been the contemporary of Wyndham Lewis and not belonged to the next generation. As it was, his whole career was buffeted by the events of his time.

Born in 1910 in Wales, Merlyn Evans grew up in Glasgow and then came to the Royal College of Art in London to study. His early work was deeply affected by surrealism, and he was one of the youngest artists to exhibit in the great London surrealist exhibition of 1936. Economic prospects for a painter in the 1930s were exceptionally poor however, so he took a teaching job in South Africa. He was there in 1939 when war broke out, and he served with the 8th Army in North Africa and in Italy before returning permanently to this country. It was not easy for him to remake his career in post-war London, and he again turned to teaching, especially at the Central School and at the Royal College of Art. He died suddenly in 1973, at the age of 63.

Merlyn's many friends and students will remember him with affection. He was an excellent teacher, who took a particular delight in showing one the possibilities of the print media, of which he was such a master. I can vividly remember conversations with him in his holiday flat overlooking Porthmeor Beach in St Ives where he loved to swim in the roughest of seas. Merlyn was a great talker who loved to explore ideas, a man for whom art was the ultimate manifestation of deeply considered feelings.

Rather than attempt a small-scale retrospective exhibition, we have chosen to concentrate on a single phase of Merlyn Evans's work, less well known today than his later abstract paintings but surely of equal interest. In the late 1930s and 1940s he painted a series of figure compositions in which he analysed the aggressive element in human nature, which was so very much in evidence during the period.

The paintings are not so much about particular historical events as about the attitude of mind behind them. They are quite unique, and retain their message today. They will complement the abstract paintings and the prints that are being shown elsewhere in London at the moment.

The exhibition was first promised by my predecessor, Sir Norman Reid. The paintings have been selected and catalogued by David Fraser Jenkins, Assistant Keeper in the Modern Collection. We are most grateful to all the lenders who have helped to make the exhibition possible, and especially to the artist's widow, the pianist Margerie Few, and to his daughter, the architect Eldred Evans.

Alan Bowness *Director*

Acknowledgements

I am grateful to Merlyn Evans's friends of long standing who have talked about him with me: F.E. McWilliam, Hal Missingham, Thelma Hulbert and Morris Kestelman. In South Africa his first wife, Phyl Behrman, kindly replied to written queries, and both she and Jill Addleson at the Durban Art Gallery found early newspaper references. Lars Rostrup Boyesen at the Royal Museum of Fine Arts, Copenhagen, provided information on his contacts there. Bryan Robertson's catalogue of his mid-career retrospective exhibition at the Whitechapel Art Gallery in 1956 has been a frequent reference book. I would also like to thank Eldred Evans, William Gear, Madeleine Ponsonby, Eugene Rosenberg, Michael Servaes, Hugh T. Stevenson, Angela Weight and most especially Margerie Evans.

David Fraser Jenkins

Introduction

The title of this exhibition needs qualification: not all the paintings here are political. The earliest ones are not, but are included as it is essential to display some of Merlyn Evans's first abstract paintings. It was the lack of relevance of his landscape and still life painting to the desperate social situation in Glasgow in 1930, according to his own account, which caused him to look for something new and to start his own 'abstract drawings of a timid personal kind'. His abstract painting was linked in this way to his own daily experience, and it was this dislike of suffering that became fundamental to his later 'political' painting. He was never interested in promoting any party or doctrine, but he had seen how atrociously people could behave to one another during the depression in Glasgow, and he grew up to be aware of the increasing cruelty and menace that finally became the war. This pessimism about personal behaviour he saw confirmed in international disputes, and his paintings often identify individual and national conflicts. There is also in the title a cut off point by date, and only works of the 1930s and 40s are exhibited. The most clearly political of all Evans's paintings is 'The Meeting' of 1951, a large oil (painted for the Festival of Britain exhibition, *60 Paintings for '51*) of workers showing hands at an open air meeting of the Electrical Trades Union. The date limit is justified in this case as it is a painting of a different character from the wartime work – the subject is no longer humanity in general at its least humane, it is less violent and in appearance is more open in composition. 'The Meeting', and even some of the later abstract paintings, are also political, but remain to be the subject of another exhibition.

Most of the paintings here are of the war, yet Merlyn Evans was not an official war artist. The pictures that now belong to the Imperial War Museum, for example, have only recently gone there. Since they were not painted for submission to a committee in London, and since Sapper Evans had the same direct experience of war as his fellow engineers, he drew on a greater personal commitment to the subject. Of all the major British artists who painted the last war, he is the only one to have consistently carried on using the same advanced style that was already his before the war.

Evans was regarded as a prodigy at the Glasgow School of Art, no doubt mostly because of his skill in drawing. This skill, as much scientific as artistic, persisted through his life, and his works are always recognisable by their precision in outline. He was encouraged to compete for the Rome Scholarship, and followed the renaissance-like routine of mural designs and life studies. He did not win (the award went to subsequently forgotten artists in the two years he competed) and he went instead to the Royal College of Art in London from 1932 to 1934. He had acquired a style like Crivelli or Signorelli, but turned this into something more of his own time by making crystalline landscapes slightly in the manner of Stanley Spencer. He had already begun to make abstract work as well. Evans's exemplars of abstraction were found in *Cahiers d'Art* and other art magazines, and also in a monograph on sculpture and drawings by the Vorticist Lawrence Atkinson (1873–1931). Atkinson's planar network of elegant lines in relief is echoed in Evans's three early sculptures on display and also in such paintings of 1934 as 'The Conquest of Time'. From the beginning, however, there was some real subject at the origin of these, revealed at times by the artist's own notes made for later exhibitions. One of the most resistant to visual reading is the earliest painting in the exhibition, 'Vertical Crustacean' (1930). A later gloss by the artist explains that it was derived from the shapes of a leaf and a prawn, in so far, evidently, as they corresponded to his own delicate line. The origins of such an image are in the microscope, and hence the unconventionality of its appearance. 'Beechwood by Moonlight' and 'The Conquest of Time', are similarly based on natural observation, although more complex and sculptural in character.

From 1934 the more important of his paintings were inspired by current affairs. The subject is never explicit, except by topicality. Noticing that the date of 'The Chess Players' is 1940, one might guess that it refers to the signing of the non-aggression pact between Hitler and Stalin – but in principle it could refer to some other treaty, and would in that case still remain as powerful. The only certainty is that what is represented is evil. Evans's pessimism about human nature, at least in international life, is from then always evident, and his subjects are abstracted to this general level. The figures perform on a stage, as in a renaissance altarpiece, and although the forms are very different the presentation continues the method of the mural studies submitted for the Rome Scholarship. It also comes close to Wyndham Lewis's technique during the 1930s.

This attraction to Lewis was in the first place literary, both for his independence of attitude and the aggressive style of his writing. This literariness extends to his paintings which, at least in theory, can be expounded item by item. During the war, when Evans was at times unable to paint, he would work out the composition of his next painting in words, and make written notes in a pocket book stating what the various parts would represent. Evans did not see an exhibition of Lewis's work until December 1937 (and did not meet him until after the war), although he must have known of his work before this, and there is a connection between his 'Suppliants' of 1934 and Lewis's 'Group of Suppliants' of the year before. In his first works in South Africa, and perhaps just before this (these paintings were destroyed in London during the war), Evans loosened the cubist structure of his paintings so as to depict the protagonists as hard surfaced, partly abstract humanoids. These owe something to Lewis's contemporary work, although they are idiosyncratic in their graphic construction. Evans was sensitive to the comparison with Lewis, not because of fear of plagiarism – for they are not all that similar – but because before the war Lewis was hated for his right-wing political sympathies. Evans disliked joining any artists' or political group, but was closer to socialism than to any other political theory, and was never at all on the right. His admiration for Lewis was counter to his politics, which in Lewis's case were hardly appreciable in his painted work.

With his wife and two young children Evans emigrated to South Africa in May 1938. He went because he had found a good teaching job in Durban, and he despaired of exhibiting or selling his work in London. The recent death of his mother had also been a great personal distress. In Durban he arranged his first exhibition, which although it had no catalogue was extensively reviewed, and he sold work, both semi-abstract and more conventional landscapes and portraits. Neither he nor his wife had connections in South Africa, but he came to know a number of painters in Durban, particularly Alex Wagner, who were interested in contemporary art.

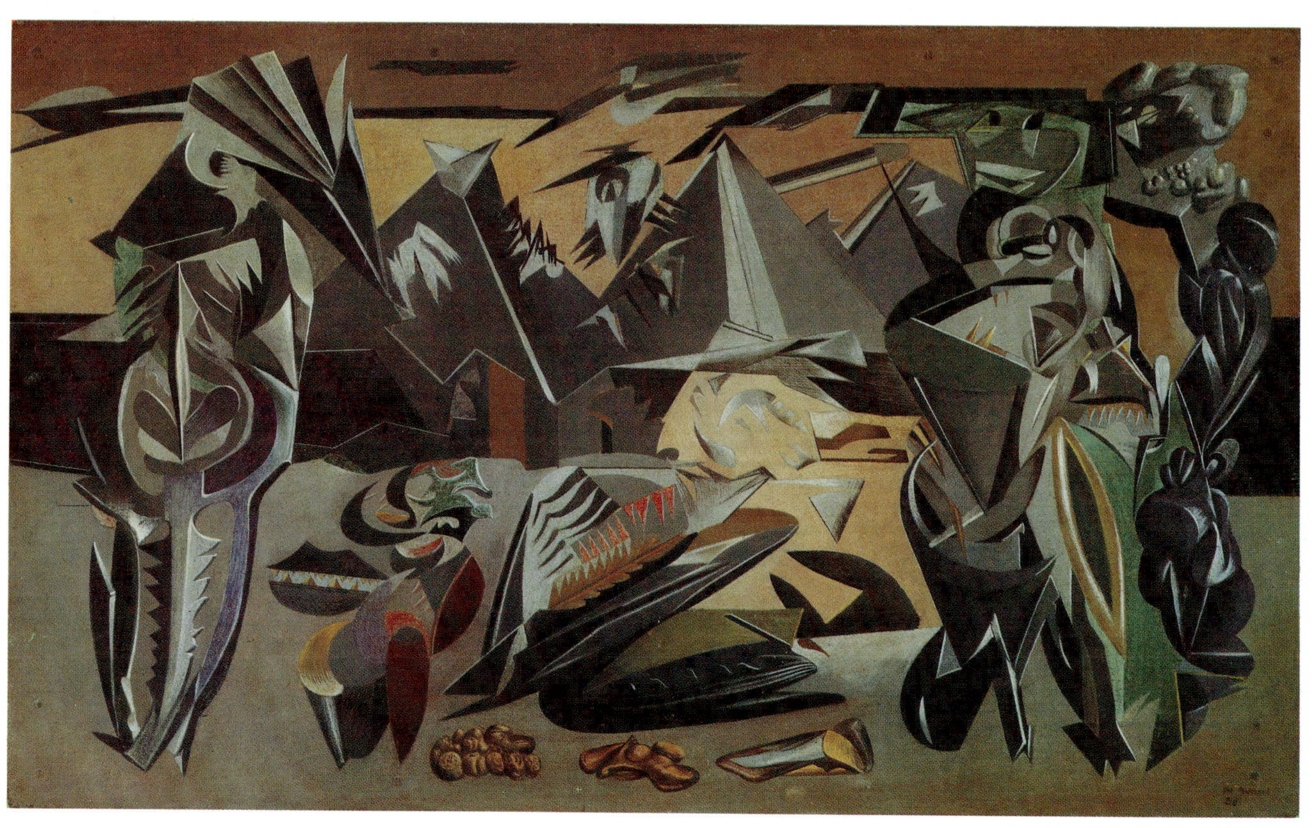

Distressed Area
February 1938
(cat.no.9)

The Crucifixion 1945
(cat.no.27)

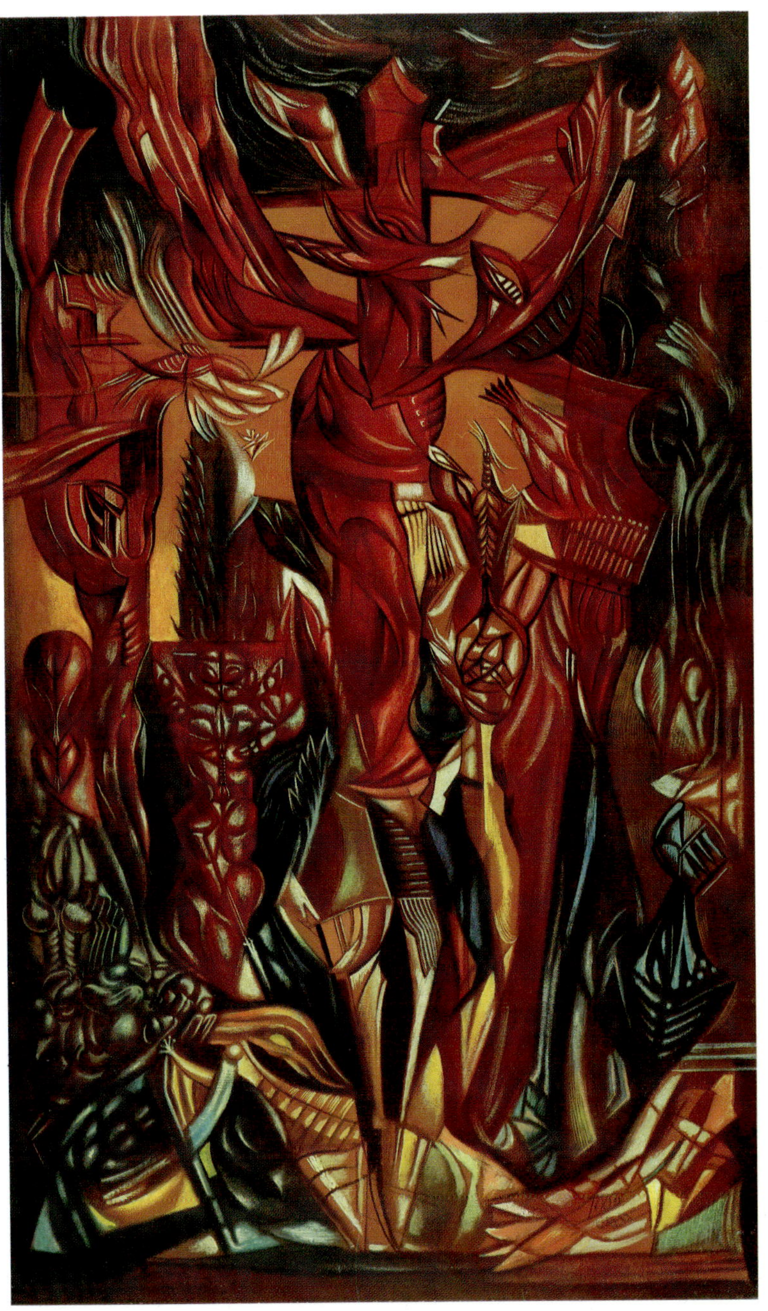

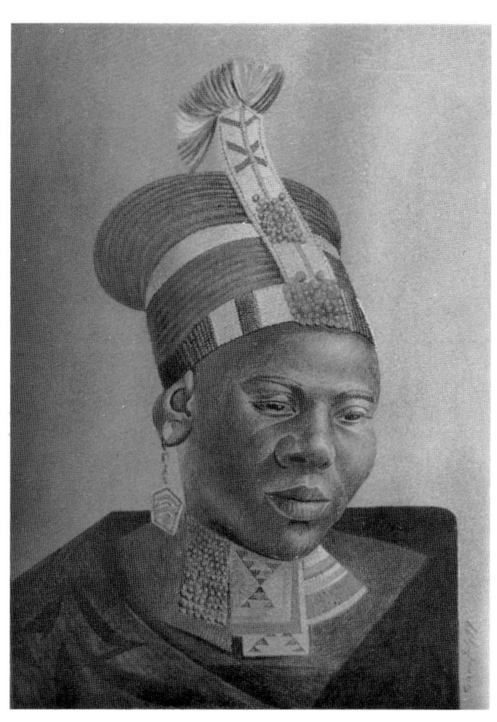

Zulu Woman July 1939
Tempera on board, $18\frac{1}{4} \times 14$ (46.3 × 35.5)
Durban Art Gallery, South Africa

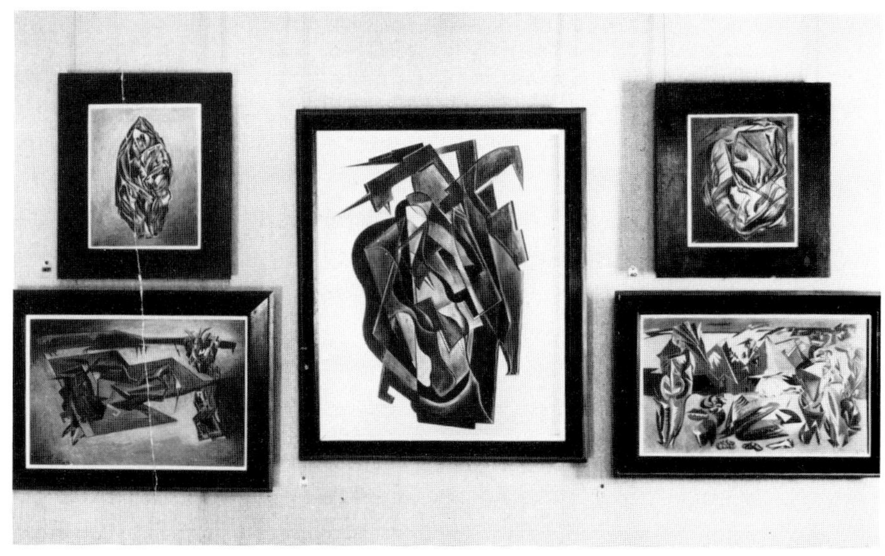

Paintings by Merlyn Evans
at 'Abstract Paintings by 9
British Artists', Lefevre Gallery,
March 1939

The 'Distressed Area', which has to do with the Spanish Civil War, was painted early in 1938 before he left London. The Durban newspapers mention the titles of paintings exhibited the following July, some of them brought out from Britain and others painted in South Africa (most of these have remained in public and private collections in that country): 'Tyrannopolis' (later called 'The Protestors'), 'Massacre of the Innocents', 'Summer Evening', 'Garden in Durban', 'Dance of Death', 'The Solipsist', 'Crime without Passion', 'Judith and Holofernes with the Infant Hercules', 'Freud adoring Laius & Worshipping the Sphinx', 'Encounter between Laius & Electra'.

In 1940–1 Evans invented a group of paintings on war subjects, all of them condemnations of aggression. It is the immorality of individuals that is depicted, but in such abstract terms that the problem is general. The natural expressive language of the shapes of beaks, flames, teeth, hand positions and positions within the rectangular painting, worked out in the paintings and drawings of the earlier 1930s, is now exploited fluently. The extreme pessimism of these paintings was recognised by the artist, but considered well justified by the situation of war. In a private letter of November 1944 he explained this:

'Now T.E. Hulme, a man for whom I have a somewhat immoderate admiration . . . was very aware of the kind of complications which face us at present, and he was at pains as you will remember to refute the unquestioned and generally accepted post-renaissance humanist concept that man is naturally *good*. He drew attention to the dogma of original sin . . . At that time such an idea was very difficult to get across, like the elements of cruelty and violence which are to be found in many of my paintings. Now – we have no trouble in agreeing that humanity is very wicked *indeed* . . . the principle employed by Hulme is important, viz. to attack the great *unconscious* (in the non-psychological sense) general assumptions, such as the desirability of progress per se; the Hedonist-Humanist concept (in a time of unparalleled misery) that the end of human life is happiness for the many.'

Merlyn Evans returned to London after the war as a South African artist, and exhibited as such in the group show in the Tate Gallery in September 1948. His first one-man exhibition in London was not until the following year in the Leicester Galleries. He was then aged thirty-nine, and this debut had been delayed by the war. Some of the war paintings were displayed, along with a quantity of post-war work (a full retrospective came only in 1956 at the Whitechapel Gallery). It must have been apparent that here was an artist quite untouched by the neo-romanticism of the 1940s, or by the illustrational style of the official war artists. His friend Roy Campbell, the South African poet, wrote the short introduction in the Leicester Gallery catalogue. He recognised Evans's aim as 'the tragic reality' devoid of superficial attractions. The origin of his painting Roy Campbell placed in the 'world of men and events and the mythology that weaves itself into the patterns of their behaviour'. The mythology is not explicit, as it had sometimes been in his painting before the war, and in the exhibition only 'Prometheus' and 'The Crucifixion' had such subjects. The patterns of behaviour exposed by Evans exist as visible patterns in his compositions. The symbols accumulated in some paintings draw on his knowledge of Egyptian and other primitive arts, and combine with quite personal recollections. Sometimes the Christian subjects of old master paintings are hinted at, and in the partly abstract works these echo to broaden the relevance of his subject.

In 1936 Evans had listed his own name with other British artists whose attitude 'strikes a balance between Mondrian or Dali, or opens the way to an art which gives due recognition to the dignity of subjects and the status of the Picture Object'. Such a balance between abstraction and violent subject matter was unique to Merlyn Evans in his comments on the international politics of the 1940s.

Merlyn Evans's Use of Egg Tempera

Merlyn Evans was by nature a craftsman. As he recalled: 'my parents . . . considered that I was probably too practical with my hands to be a potential artist'. However, this is an essential attribute of the artist intent on using the medium of egg tempera, which involves a high degree of craft skill, from the priming of the support to the preparation and methodical application of the paint.

Used in a traditional manner the medium suits the artist with a clear conception of the results he wishes to achieve and a strong sense of draughtsmanship and design. The attractions of the medium and its history led to a revival of its use towards the end of the nineteenth century in England. This was largely through the efforts of the members of the Arts and Crafts movement based in Birmingham. Apart from those artists fortunate enough to gain experience in Italy, technical information was mainly derived from Cennino Cennini's *Il Libro dell'Arte, Trattato della Pittura* written near the beginning of the fifteenth century in Italy and translated into English in 1844 by Mrs Merrifield. Birmingham artists such as Joseph Southall and Maxwell Armfield were enthusiastic exponents of the medium followed by many others such as Edward Wadsworth. Abroad, Giorgio de Chirico was one of the few artists using tempera whose work Evans knew.

Merlyn Evans's interest in the medium was probably first aroused by the Italian tempera painters of the fourteenth and fifteenth centuries. In the early 1930s he made a finished copy of a Madonna and Child by Crivelli. Tempera soon became his favourite medium for abstract work, which he used frequently until he joined the army during the Second World War. He was still using tempera after his discharge in 1946. His widow, Margerie Evans, remembers that when they shared a flat with several friends in Mecklenburgh Square, the precious ration of fresh eggs disappeared on one occasion, almost causing the eviction of the painter.

Like many artists who are also avid readers, it is likely that Evans acquired much of his technical knowledge from books. In 1927 *The Technique of Painting* by

C. Moreau Vauthier was awarded to him as first prize for art by the Allen Glen's School in Glasgow. This contains only a small section on tempera painting, but it is known that he possessed several other books on technique.

Pure egg tempera paint consists of pigments ground in water to the consistency of a stiff paste, to which is added diluted yolk of egg as a binder. It dries in seconds after application, defying further manipulation, and will crack if applied too thickly. For these reasons the paint film has to be painstakingly built up with numerous discrete brushstrokes. This produces the characteristic 'hatched' application visible on many tempera paintings.

In 'Vertical Crustacean' 1930 (cat.no.1) Evans has employed this method to develop the modelling in some parts of the central image. More generally however he has applied broad washes of colour which required the paint to be appreciably thinned with water. The extreme thinness of these diluted tempera films is revealed by the visibility of the pencilled grid below, drawn to assist the transfer of his original design to the panel.

'Polynesian Fantasy' 1935 (cat.no.10) was probably painted with a modified egg medium. Egg yolk is a complex emulsion of fats and oils dispersed in water which, when used as a binder in paint, dries to form a tough and durable film. It contains a considerable excess of emulsifier which allows more than its own weight of oily substances to be added. The addition of oils (e.g. linseed oil) and/or dissolved resins (e.g. dammar in turpentine) to produce a paint with handling properties more akin to those of oil paint was common practice amongst the tempera revivalists. Such modified temperas allow the application of thicker and more broadly worked passages, as in the green background of 'Polynesian Fantasy'. Analysis of this layer has shown the presence of egg, while under magnification undispersed clumps of pigment are clearly visible, typical of a studio preparation. (Pigment particles in industrially manufactured paints are uniformly dispersed in the medium by the action of roller mills.)

In the same way that Evans varied the formulations of his paint, he also changed the manner in which he prepared his painting supports. Traditionally, a wood panel is given about twelve coats of gesso made from specially prepared gypsum in animal glue size. The complete process is lengthy, and requires both patience and skill; consequently artists sought simpler alternatives. Evans was no exception.

'Vertical Crustacean' is painted on a water soluble ground consisting mainly of lithopone, which is an intimate mixture of barium sulphate and zinc sulphide (identified by x-ray diffraction and spectographic analysis by Ashok Roy of the National Gallery, London). Lithopane is more commonly found in cheap mass-produced paints. The ground was applied to a finely woven linen canvas stretched over a wooden panel. The panel provides rigidity to the otherwise flexible canvas to prevent the brittle ground from cracking.

'Polynesian Fantasy' is painted on strawboard to which a piece of muslin had been glued before being primed with a ground, now insoluble in water. Perhaps this is bound with casein (a binder derived from milk) which was recommended for preparing grounds by Max Doerner whose influential book first appeared in English in 1934. Gluing a piece of fine canvas to the panel face before applying the gesso was recommended by Cennini. It provides a good base for the gesso, evening out any imperfections and guarding against defects resulting from knots or joins.

Although the sense of involvement with his materials would have appealed to Evans's craftsmanlike nature, it was the quality of line and clarity of image obtainable with egg tempera that primarily attracted him to it. Referring to his early abstract paintings in his 1956 Whitechapel Gallery exhibition catalogue he wrote 'I have always preferred the medium of tempera, which is particularly suited to sharply defined forms.' Despite this insistence on clearly realised forms he did not make full use of the purity and luminosity of colour, prized by tempera painters and exemplified in the work of artists such as Wadsworth. However, in keeping with the craft traditions of tempera was Evans's careful construction of all his own frames to complete the process of making his painting, and to provide adequate protection to the delicate paint surface.

Evans produced few works in the medium after 1940, initially perhaps because of complications with the technique during war service. Following the Second World War, he began to work more often on a larger scale and almost completely abandoned the medium, although he always retained the precision of line and form reminiscent of his earlier work in egg tempera.

Background   *Merlyn Evans, 1956*

1913 family left Cardiff where I was born and moved to Glasgow, where I got to know ships and the Clydeside. At an early age fascinated by ships, their colour, design and rigs, from the point of view of their shape and colour. We had at home a book of engraved illustrations illustrating the history of ships, and also one illustrating sections of cargo boats. I later procured one on various designs of racing craft and at the age of twelve to fourteen I started to make model yachts. In Glasgow this was and is a sport for men, and the models are five foot or six foot long. To this activity I allied an interest in kite design and flying, and made numerous formal variations.

These activities, together with the many hours I spent drawing white fantail pigeons, I now see as providing a particular bias in favour of my subsequent preoccupation with art and, at the still youngish age of seventeen, with abstract form. I used to enjoy looking at mechanical engineering drawings and enjoyed looking at machinery. This my parents considered quite inconsistent with my love of painting and drawing, and considered that I was probably too practical with my hands to be a potential 'artist'. So I was sent to a school which was noted for training mechanics, engineers, chemists and physicists, etc. However these subjects presented in mathematical formulae meant nothing to me – and I eventually spent all my time in the art room, where I was encouraged to copy reproductions of Constable's 'Hayfield' and Raeburn's 'Boy with a Rabbit', and also watercolours in the Kelvingrove Museum. The art room contained volumes of the *Studio*, and I spent my lunch hours going through these old numbers till I nearly knew them by heart. I passed Matric. and it was agreed that I go to Glasgow Art School, then presided over by J.D. Revel. Prior to this I had private tuition from John and Charles Houston. John was a Royal Scottish Academician and Charles was R.S.W.S., and they gave me lessons for nothing, and taught me to admire Israels, Whistler and Sickert, and to paint by values. In 1920 John Houston was over seventy, Charles, sixty-five. They were immersed in the plein-airism of the Barbizon School, and could just manage to take Whistler, but not the Post-Impressionists. They made me go out in the fields at all times of the day and paint from nature. I also attempted portraiture and still life.[1]

By 1925–6 I began to see an ugly side of life as I travelled through the bad part of Glasgow every day to school. The General Strike took place, and looting and violence were daily occurrences. The crowd, the mob, went unhindered through the streets, and a student who was driving a tram car was torn to pieces by women at Bridgetown Cross. All transport in the streets ran the gauntlet of stoning. My work continued to be of a lyrical nature and I worked in various styles of artists I admired. Alex Reid and Lefèvre staged the first big show of modern art that Glasgow had seen. It was held at the Maclellan Galleries, and included the large Douanier Rousseau of orange trees with monkeys, a large Lurçat and some small Picassos in the neoclassical period of 1926.[2]

By 1930 unemployment was bad, slums in Glasgow were bad, and ill health among the poor was general. Gangs of young men armed with coshes, razors and so forth had open fights in the streets. Wall Street in America collapsed, financiers suicided, and the German reichmark became worthless. By this time I had begun some abstract drawings of a timid personal kind. Conventional painting of any kind seemed inappropriate in the world in which I lived. It also seemed unlikely that I should ever earn my living as an artist. The only pictures that were bought were those which to me had no meaning at all.

I was overcome with a strong sense of futility, collapse and sterility in general affairs. Unknown to me the response abroad had been Dada and Surrealism. My work at this time took the form of drawings and tempera paintings which were ideographs and formal inventions and contrivances, sometimes organic in character and usually a single image. I won a scholarship of £50, which seemed a fortune to me at that time as my pocket money was two shillings a week.

I went to Berlin and stayed in a hotel near the station in Inverlidenstrasse. I studied some very fine Chinese paintings at, I believe, the Kaiser Frederick Museum. This 11th–12th century Chinese work impressed me greatly. I also saw an important exhibition by Feininger, and work by Klee and Kandinsky at, I think, Galerie Flechtheim. There was a huge show of modern art at Schloss Plas, a kind of

Palace – some of the work shown was trivial and bad. As one went about the streets there was the sound of an occasional shot. Hitler's men were shooting the police, and the Communists were shooting the police. Berlin was lecherous and poverty ridden. Crowds of half starved, ill dressed, ugly women roamed the streets at night. They looked tired, hopeless and aimless.[3]

I went to Copenhagen where the situation was reversed, and everything was gay, happy and healthy. I painted a number of pictures, of which two were exhibited and the rest left over there. My half-cousin the painter Mathias Koedt was a successful Danish artist, who worked in a manner between that of Munch and Van Gogh.[4] He had a huge and magnificent studio in which were vast easels, a litho press and enormous pictures. He mixed sand with his paint which, he told me, was carefully purified of salts. This sand enabled him to develop a formidable impasto like that of de Stael, and like de Stael he applied the paint with trowels and knives. I didn't like his pictures at all. Mathias advised me to go to the Glyptotek (the Carlsberg beer endowment) to study the work of Denmark's greatest artist, Wilumsen. There was a great deal of Wilumsen's work there, and it was fulsome and pretentious. There was an enormous relief that took up the wall of a room, and used every material from granite to marble and gilded bronze. It ranged from low relief to high practically free-standing relief, and was a display of excess and vulgarity that was much admired. There was a considerable collection of early impressionist works by Gauguin, which surprised me, and a very excellent series of paintings by Juan Gris.[5] I liked these very much, revisited them a number of times and regretted that they were not entirely abstract. I spent a long time in con-versation with my cousin Peske Koedt, who was a musician, persuading him that abstract art must eventually succeed. He finally commissioned and bought a picture from me, which enabled me to stay longer. I returned to Paris, saw some more work by Kandinsky and some paintings by Lurçat of sailing ships' masts, presenting a crazy and chaotic scene of masts, sails and rigging, being blown to pieces in a storm. These were painted (or shown) in New York at the time of the economic blizzard. I found them unpleasant in colour, form and handling, but expressive. I also saw work by Miro, which struck me as a comedian's rendering of Kandinsky, and resembled astrological charts. There were on view small gouaches by Chirico, horses 'se cabrant devant la mer', and some antiquarian pictures by

Campigli, carefully patinated to look old. There were also some lugubrious paintings by Tchelitchew.

I met Georges Maratier of Galerie Vignon, then run by Mme. Cutoli. She was showing rugs by Léger, Picasso, Rouault, etc. Maratier liked the look of the photographs of paintings which I had done in Denmark and urged me to stay in Paris, but my family would not agree, and I returned to Glasgow, and sent Maratier a few paintings which he showed.

I took a teaching course on which my parents were determined, but escaped by winning a scholarship to the Royal College – this was £80 a year. At that time the College was run by Sir William Rothenstein and abstract art was severely discouraged. I asked to be taught sculpture – this was refused. I had already had five years of art schools, colleges, etc. I practised sculpture in the back yard of my lodgings under the tuition of Mr Cobbold, a stone mason, and worked at drawing and tempera paintings in my bedroom. These were shown to MacDonald of Alex Reid and Lefèvre, who considered the work too cerebral and lacking in sensuality. I resigned from the College after a year, got a job and continued to work on my own. At that time, 1933, Nicholson was working à la Braque, Lewis was doing portraits, Wadsworth meticulous tempera marine pieces and still life paintings, and Surrealism began to cross the Channel. An anti-abstract revolt was taking place in Paris. Dali wrote of the constructivists as presenting 'the warmed-up soup of neo-Kantianism, . . . gluant de sections d'or'.[6] Moore contrived to be undisturbed and to unite the two extremes, as did Paul Nash. I was invited to show at the 1936 Surrealist Exhibition and attended numerous meetings at the home of Roland Penrose, where Herbert Read presided and Humphrey Jennings introduced Courbet and social realism, and read the obiter dicta of Radek the Stalin art dictator.

I refused to be implicated politically, and left. The group later disintegrated over the Stalin/Trotsky issue, and Aragon joined the Party. Lewis had come out strongly against Surrealism in 'The Diabolical Principle and the Dythyrambic Spectator' and later 'Men Without Art'. In 1936 he showed in the Leicester Galleries – these were the first paintings of his I had seen.[7] At this time I was doing a series of paintings and drawings inspired by Freudian theories, which reveal the influence of Surrealism.

In 1937 I painted a large abstract picture called 'The Massacre of the Innocents' and in the same year 'Blind Beggars', 'Gopher Diamonds', 'Disturbance in the East' and 'Distressed Area'. I also produced some abstract polychrome reliefs inspired by Egyptian wall painting and coffin painting. In this year my mother committed suicide.[8] I left for South Africa in the spring of 1938, hoping to see Egypt.

I arrived in South Africa in the hot season, and settled in Durban in Natal. Violent colour burst on the senses with a harsh, raucous trumpeting. The light was merciless, continuous and blinding. Vermilion and veridian trees and bushes, magenta hedges, and a monotonous blue sky that was always the same produced to my eyes hideous dissonances of colour which fascinated me, as in England I would admire the copper glow as the sky would light up in the evening with a blast furnace. The following year war was declared, and in the next year Hitler made a pact with Stalin. At this period the following pictures emerged: 'Conflict', 'The Lock', 'The Mark of the Beast', 'The Entombment', 'The Chess Players', 'The Calumniators', 'Tyrranopolis' and 'Puppet Government'. Portraits were made of Zulus, Pondo women and Basutos. I copied bushmen rock drawings for the Witz Museum, and spent time doing stone carving and learning to cast in bronze. I also did portraits of a number of Europeans, which did not appeal as they were lacking in sentiment. I painted a large mural in the Clubhouse of Natal Technical College – 8′ × 70′. This was recently destroyed.

In August 1942 I joined the South African Army 14th Armoured Brigade Signals Company. While training to be a wireless operator in the tank regiment, the picture called 'Entombment' was painted. It contained memories of my mother's burial, local Hindu cremation ceremonies, yacht racing on Durban Bay, armoured molochs and harsh raucous tropical colour. In the centre two vultures stand in the portico of a small imitation Greek temple such as the Natal Indians like to build.

After six months of hard training it was discovered that I could lecture, and I was suddenly transferred to the Engineers, to a remote camp outside Pretoria called Spitz Kop. During my leave to Johannesburg once a fortnight for twenty-four hours I contrived to paint one picture called 'Nocturnal Fantasy', the subject matter and details of which I wrote down before I painted it. It contained memories of a truncated conical hill against which are the vague forms of African native soldiers watching an open air cinema, and below which an asbestos miner pushes a truck. In the foreground is a puppet, wearing a mask of the kind used in New Ireland. The

other smaller figures have the stylised silhouettes of the carvings from the French
Kameruns, North Africa. The air is full of locusts, on the right is a dummy tree of
the type used by infantry snipers.

In 1943 I was transferred to a field company of the Engineers and joined Section
One, a front line detachment. I realised my ambition and found myself in Egypt and
Libya. While in Tobruk on a decoy operation where we worked always at night and
rested during the light hours, I painted two pictures, 'Souvenir of Tobruk', which
depicts a massed group of figures on the beach of Tobruk Bay, and 'Nocturnal
Drama' in which there are memories of an allegorical and symbolical kind, and the
subject of which was written out beforehand, since although I had imagined the
picture I did not have time to work at it immediately. These two works were
transferred by plane to Johannesburg where they were shown at the annual show.

The Allies struck through Normandy and not on the Turkish border as the
Germans had been led to expect, and we were sent to Taranto to take part in the
Italian Campaign. While stationed behind the lines in San Arcangelo near Rimini,
which had been entirely smashed, to pass the time during the day (our activities
again being always at night) I collected some local white clay while we were
digging-in telegraph poles. With this clay I made a portrait of the section officer,
Capt. Nicolai, an Africaner. This was exhibited in some art exhibition run by the
8th Army, to which I belonged. I was next moved in the advance to Ravenna,
where in charge of a squad of Italian prisoners I ran a stores dump supplying the
line troops, which in this section were Polish. At my request the section officer, in
consideration of my isolation, procured during a leave to Rome a new and a very
good copy of Dante's *Comedia* with Carey's translation. I read this through three or
more times, and now unfortunately recall little of it but intend to study it again. I
had with me besides Eliot's collected poems, works by Roy Campbell, plays by
Beaumont and Fletcher, *The Prince* by Machiavelli and *Salammbo* by Flaubert. I also
had the poems, and *Petits poèmes en Prose* by Baudelaire, and Byron's letters, and I
kept re-reading these books as they were small and took up little room.

During this time it was severe winter, snow was on the ground and we slept in
bombed-out dwellings without roofs or windows. I was next attached to Section A,
a front line decoy unit whose job it was to draw enemy fire while the real attack
was launched elsewhere. We usually started operation at 2 a.m. and worked till

dawn. Sometimes we worked during early morning, and were protected by mortar umbrellas.

Severe fighting took place at the village where Byron sent his daughter to a convent school. Bagnacavallo was retaken twice and our truck or troop carrier was set alight by incendiary shells. The large picture 'Paesaggio Tragico', inspired by the smashed landscape, the Senio river and the colours of the mosaic in Theodoric's Tomb in Ravenna, escaped as it had been left behind that night at the billet in Ravenna. Also my easel made from parts of German artillery predictors, and a paint box made from scrap wood in Tobruk which were kept in a tool locker were saved, and the picture sent back to South Africa.

During this time I painted two more works, 'The Drinker' and an allegorical picture called 'Simeon'. These were packed in twenty-five pounder shell cartons to be taken by an officer to South Africa. However he lost them in Rome, and I set to and painted them again, but they were not so good. In Ravenna I contrived to see San Vitale. The Germans had broken the pumps and the whole church was flooded with three foot of water and looked like a magnificent swimming bath. Sgt. Zeedenbung remarked that no wonder Italians were poor since they squandered their money on churches like this. I also saw . . . and from a small painting conceived an idea for a Crucifixion. The Germans gave in when we crossed the Po at Ferrara, and we helped to build the main Bailey Bridge which is still in use and one of the longest made during the war. Lifting and fitting these iron parts was heavy and dangerous work as we were some height above the river. Next I was moved to Mogliano five miles outside Venice, and encamped in Indian patrol tents in the gardens of a Palladian villa, where nightingales in profusion sang in the cherry trees at night. Here I helped clean out an Italian barracks and turn it into a British hospital, and with rolls of barbed wire, wooden stakes and mallets erect prison camps for the droves of red faced healthy German prisoners who came in daily. In spare moments in the nearby fields I finished the tempera painting of the 'Crucifixion' which is now in Nottingham Art Gallery.

In midsummer 1945 I was transferred to Rome, and attached to S.A. Headquarters in the War Records Section. I was given the rank of acting sergeant unpaid, and also asked to make portrait drawings of officers and men who had been awarded M.C. and M.M. in the S.A.E.C.[9] I made some forty of these. For three months while in Rome I studied a great deal, and made a portrait of Chirico who told me that modern painting was a débacle and that Velasquez was art, and he was trying to paint a picture in the Medici Gardens inspired by Velasquez' painting of the same subject. He was also concerned to recapture the technical and chemical secrets of the old masters and worked with gum and oil emulsions. Chirico's work had always appealed to me and had an association with my stay in Denmark where my cousin was particularly enthusiastic about 'Les Muses Inquiétants', a fine work which I later saw in Holland.

In November I was moved to London, but expected to return to South Africa and be demobilised. I arrived by Liberator having travelled from Rome in extreme discomfort wedged in the bomb rack with other men. London looked very black, foggy and grim, and after the African and Italian light I felt I lived in a nocturnal world of soft shadows and flickering lights, and not many of them.

I had work over here in store, but all but three pictures which had been left with Zwemmer were destroyed. Those left with Mesens of the London Gallery had been left by him at a Pimlico depository. It received a direct hit, and after four years of correspondence I received war damage allowance. In 1945 the Nuremburg trials took place, William Joyce the calumniator was executed, and a bomb was dropped on Hiroshima. In 1946–7 I painted 'The Execution', 'The Refugees at Spezia', 'Lovers and Street Light', 'City at Night'. These pictures were all low in tone and tightly organised in form. There were a number of pictures consequent on the 'trial' theme: 'Judge', 'Judge and Clerk', 'Conference of Mutual Distrust', 'Death of Masaryk', 'The trial of Cardinal Mindszenty', 'The Jail', 'Souvenir of Hiroshima' and 'The Atomic Landscape'. By 1950 I was making drawings of the docks near Southwark, of cranes and warehouses. There were repeated dock strikes and in 1950–1 I painted 'The Strike Meeting' of which there are three versions, and in which I tried to tackle crowd forms. The electricians' union assembled for a demonstration outside my house and disbanded later in the day outside. This produced 'Metropolitan Crowd Forming a Procession' which is now at the Festival Hall. At the same time I worked on pictures of forms in interior lighting and pictures in which luminosity and chiaroscuro play an increasingly important part. I visited Holland and studied Rembrandt. This study, together with an interest in the very remarkable drawings of Seurat, has helped me a great deal in the etchings.

My most recent work has been somewhat monochromatic in treatment owing to
the subject matter being mainly forms seen in effects of light at night. Some of them
have been somewhat looser in handling, but I have always alternated between a
free handling and a precise handling, there being no special virtue in these
activities for their own sake. Tachism, action painting and so forth are all forms of
strained Romanticism, emphasising matière, the calligraphic and cultivated
sprezzatura – i.e. counterfeit neglect.

At present I am trying to develop my studies of forms in various kinds of light,
and wish to work at the crowd motif, to which end I have made studies of the
orchestra in action at the Festival Hall and watched crowds in action where
possible.

I believe that the artist should be committed to his art only, and should avoid
allegiance to groups, isms, politics, religion or science, and that he should at least
endeavour to be free from external control as far as the times permit.

Notes

'Background' was written by Merlyn Evans for the catalogue of his exhibition at the Whitechapel
Gallery in 1956, but was not published.

1 John Houston, 1856–1932 (not in fact an RSA) and Charles Houston (exhibited at the RSA
   between 1884 and 1936) both lived in Rutherglen.
2 *A Century of French Painting* organised by Alex Reid and Lefèvre at the McLellan Galleries, May
   1927.
3 The Haldane Travelling Scholarship from Glasgow School of Art was awarded to Merlyn Evans in
   June 1931. The large Feininger exhibition was at the National-Galerie in Berlin in July. Klee and
   Kandinsky both had one-man shows at Flechtheim at other times of the year, and presumably
   Merlyn Evans saw work from stock.
4 Matthias Peschke Koedt, 1885–1949, painter of portraits and allegorical compositions,
   later editor of the magazine *Samleren*, where he took a stand against modern art.
5 One painting by Gris, 'The Guitar Player' (1926) was in the Statens Museum for Kunst, but there is
   no record of others.
6 Salvador Dali, in *La Conquête de L'Irrationnel*, Paris, 1935, in an attack on abstract painting.
7 Wyndham Lewis exhibited at the Leicester Galleries in December 1937.
8 His mother had suffered from cancer of the mouth.
9 Now in the collection of the Imperial War Museum.

Catalogue

Measurements are given in inches followed by
centimetres in brackets; height precedes width.
Works illustrated in colour are marked *

PAINTINGS AND DRAWINGS

I   Vertical Crustacean June 1930
Tempera on canvas over panel,
squared in pencil, 60 × 30
(152.5 × 76)
Inscribed lower right 'Merlyn
Evans June 1930'
First exhibited: Merlyn Evans,
Whitechapel Art Gallery,
October–November 1956 (2)
Margerie Evans

An etching of this subject, the earliest
print included in the 1972 print
retrospective exhibition at the
Victoria and Albert Museum, is also
dated 1930.
  Evans had continued to make
abstract drawings from at least the
age of seventeen, and by his own
account this developed from his
interest in technical drawings. The
origins of this design were in plant
and marine forms:
  'It is an abstraction, the forms
partly phyllomorphic and crusta-
ceomorphic' [leaf forms and crustacean forms]. 'A certain dryness and
sterility in formal character was
aimed at, the ambience, however,
bright and clear. Its original title,
which I erased, was Bright Sterility'
(1962).
  This note links his intentions in this
painting to his comment that in
Glasgow in 1930 he found that
conventional painting was intoler-
able, in view of the miserable life he
saw around him, and that in his
personal works, however timid, he
'was overcome with a strong sense of
futility, collapse and sterility' ('Background', p.21).

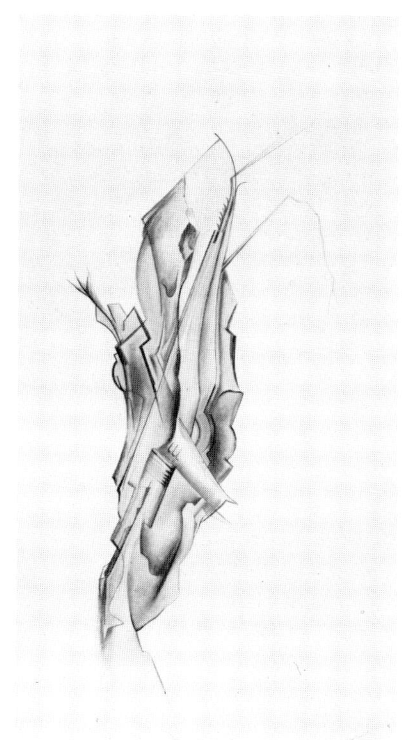

I

2   Beechwood by Moonlight
1931–3
Tempera on panel, 40 × 40
(101.5 × 101.5)
Inscribed bottom left 'Evans 33'
First exhibited: The London
Group, Royal Academy,
December–January 1945–6
National Museum of Wales

'An abstraction of lyrical character,
painted in intervals between 1931
and 1933. During evening walks in
Rutherglen I frequently passed by a

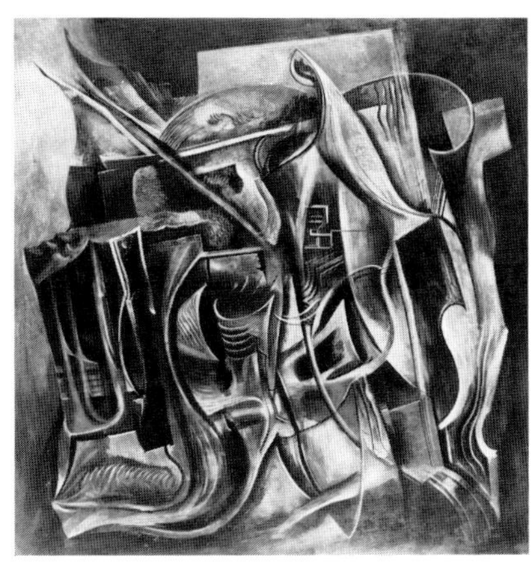

2

beechwood. The autumnal mood and colour of the picture (as well as the texture of the smooth silver beech trunks, and the crisp brown of the autumn leaves) originate from this Beechwood by Moonlight' (1962).

A finished drawing of this subject is dated 1930 (collection of Margerie Evans), and it is the painting rather than the invention which continued over the next two years. This unusual painting is an abstract landscape (hence the first title, like Whistler's, was 'Nocturne'), and despite a few background elements of design taken from 'Vertical Crustacean' (no.1) the general mood of the curves and spirals is relaxed. 'Abstraction' is used by Merlyn Evans in the literal sense that shape and colour, noticed in the subject, are designed into this overall pattern.

3 **Untitled Drawing** December 1932–January 1933
Red and black chalks on paper, squared and numbered, $25 \times 17\frac{1}{2}$ (63.5 × 44.5)
Inscribed lower right 'Evans 28 Jan 33 Dec – 32'
Margerie Evans

Evans's paintings were designed precisely in drawings before enlargement, both in the 1930s and later. This drawing resembles 'Beechwood by Moonlight' (no.2) and is a further attempt at an abstract landscape, made at a time when he was also painting quite different, completely naturalistic, landscapes.

4 **Micromorphic Study** 1933
Black ink and airbrush on paper, 30 × 22 (76 × 56)

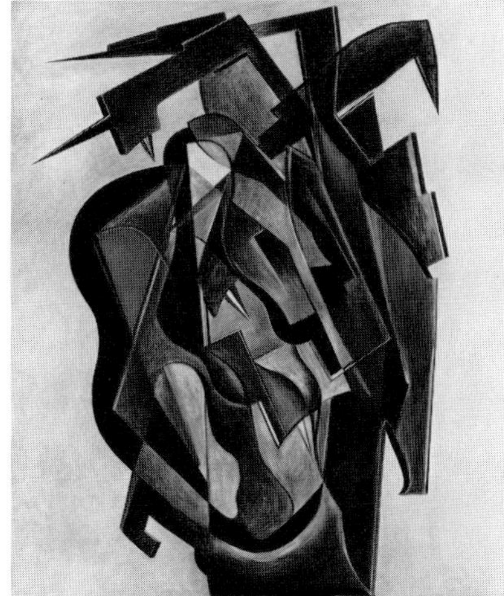

5

Not inscribed
First exhibited: probably as 'Bacterial Forms', Merlyn Evans, Whitechapel Art Gallery, October–November 1956 (81)
Margerie Evans

The title and date are taken from a photograph marked, much later, by the artist. Evans made a number of airbrush drawings in the mid 1930s, intended as finished works and not studies for paintings. They continue to exploit the direct reading of shapes, in this case microscopic, but in a more naturalistic way closer to surrealism than cubism.

5 **The Conquest of Time** 1934
Tempera and oil on canvas over panel, squared in pencil, 40 × 32 (102.5 × 81)
Inscribed lower right 'Evans 34'
First exhibited: International Surrealist Exhibition, New Burlington Galleries, June–July 1936 (98)
Tate Gallery

An engraving of this subject is also dated 1934.

This has become the best known of the early paintings since its illustration in Herbert Read's 'Surrealism' (1936) and in the 'International Surrealist Bulletin' (September 1936). Evans was not committed to the surrealist group in London however, and this is not one of his more surrealist works. He wrote to the Tate Gallery in 1967 that the image was a kingfisher 'still beside the moving river'. This links it to his belief in the parallel of natural and mechanical forms, since the upper shapes also resemble cranes:

'Derricks and cranes, and dock-side

machinery, had a fierce, heavy –
sometimes predatory – feeling;
whereas the forms of human beings,
certain birds, yachts and gliders had a
light, resilient, graceful character. I do
not mean that I saw all these things
as personages with quasi-human
attributes. The emotional qualities
were in the shapes themselves'
(Whitechapel Art Gallery catalogue,
1956, p.6).

The same contrast is evident in this
painting, and the interior, more
rounded image perhaps represents a
figure.

The title is contemporary and is so
listed in the surrealist exhibition
catalogue, and reflects the ambitious
and arcane character of many of the
other titles listed there. According to
the same note to the Tate Gallery it
seems to refer both to the image of the
bird, which is beyond Time by virtue
of the contrast with the flowing river,
and to the style itself, perhaps because
of the intention of direct communi-
cation by shape.

6   **Time King (Vertical Abstraction)**
     March 1934
     Tempera on canvas over panel,
     74 × 48 (188 × 122)
     Inscribed lower left 'March IXX /
     34 / Evans'
     First exhibited: Merlyn Evans,
     Whitechapel Art Gallery,
     October–November 1956 (9)
     Private Collection

This is the largest of Evans's pre-war
paintings. The composition reappears as (or was enlarged from) the
central section of a small tempera
painting of the same date titled 'The
Meeting', where it resembles a figure
or figures in front of a crowd.

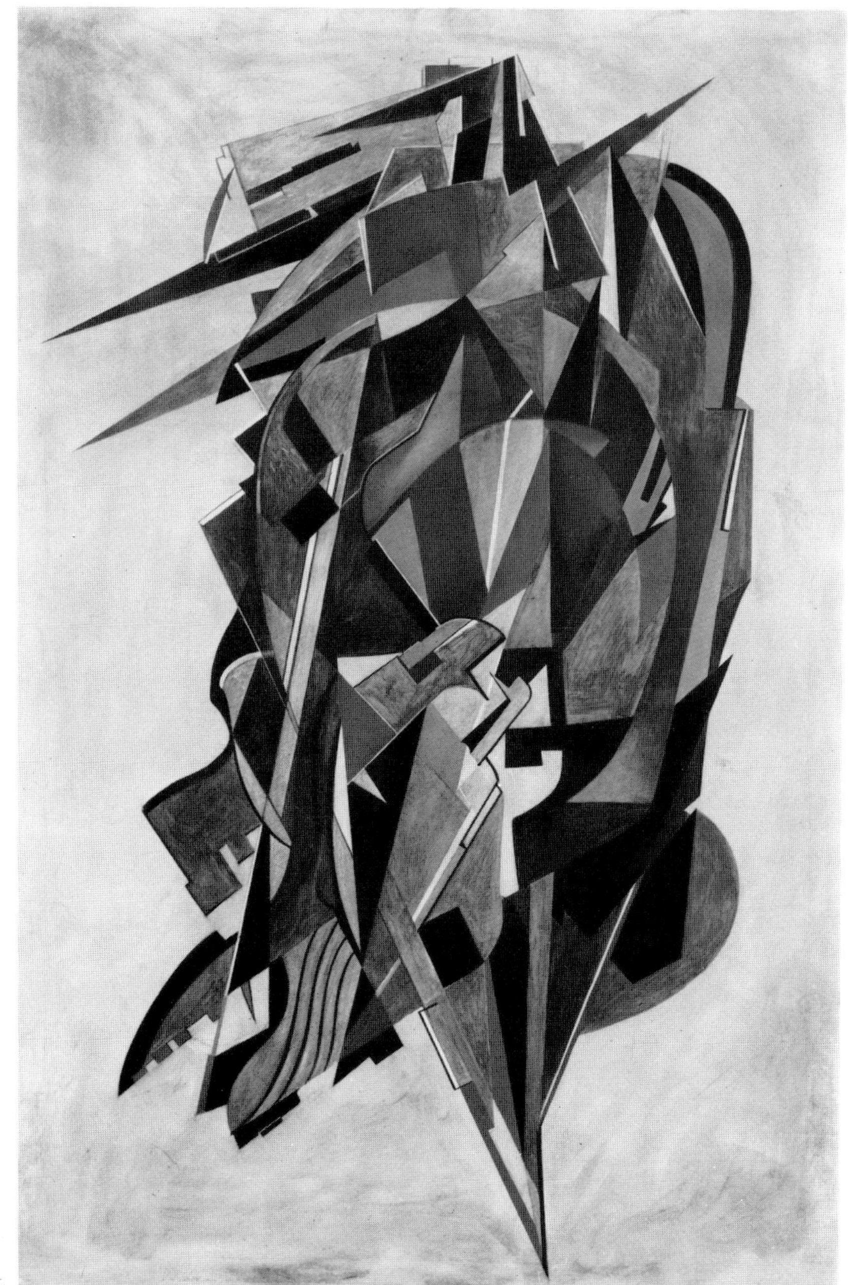

6

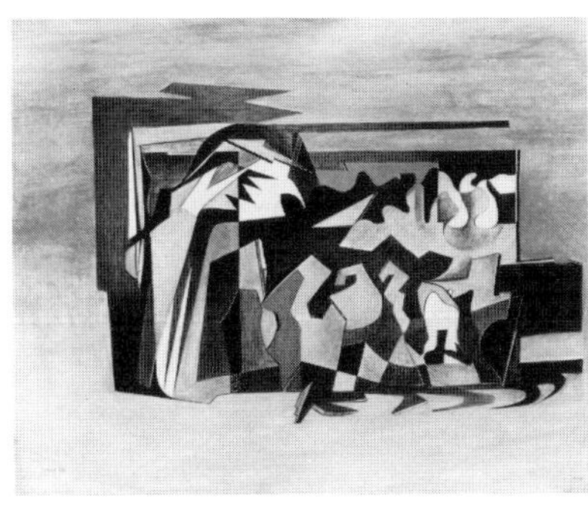

7

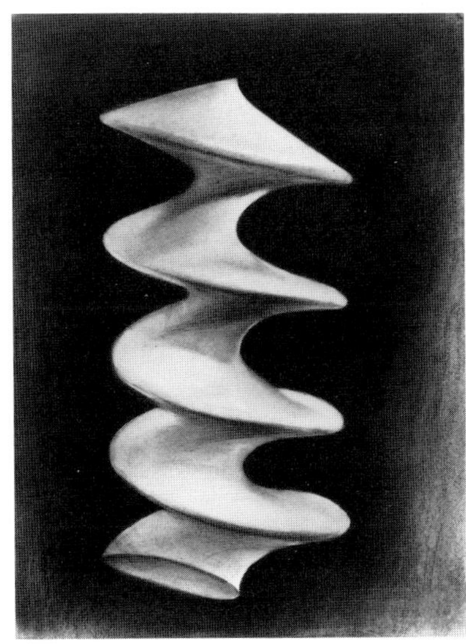

8

7   The Suppliants 1934
Tempera on canvas, 18 × 22
(45.5 × 56)
Inscribed lower left 'Evans 34'
and lower right 'Evans 1934 /
1934'
First exhibited: Merlyn Evans,
Whitechapel Art Gallery,
October–November 1956 (11).
Margerie Evans

'The Suppliants' and 'The Meeting' of
1934 are the first of Evans's paintings
that possibly refer to political events of
the day, although there is no clue to
any particular subject. The titles were
first recorded at the Whitechapel Art
Gallery exhibition in 1956, and
probably indicate at least the original
intention, if not the title, that would
have been used had they been exhibited before the war. This title may
follow Wyndham Lewis's painting
'Group of Suppliants' (1933). Lewis's
painting is of manikin figures and
quite different in appearance –
although of a type that influenced
Evans later – and the two artists met
for the first time only after the war.

This direction was not followed in
Evans's work until 1938, to judge
from drawings and the titles of
exhibited work, which reflected his
interest in Freud (most of his paintings from the mid 1930s were destroyed during the war).

8   Geometric Form (Helix) 1935
Black chalk on paper, 30 × 22
(76 × 56)
Not inscribed
First exhibited: Merlyn Evans,
Whitechapel Art Gallery,
October–November 1956 (89)
Margerie Evans

One of a number of studies of solid
geometry, some of which were taken
from photographs of three-dimen-
sional mathematical models.

***9   Distressed Area** February 1938
Tempera on canvas over panel,
18 × 36 (45.5 × 91.5)
Inscribed lower right, 'M. Evans
38' and on reverse 'begun Feb 1st
38 / 1/2/38 / Finished Feb 26 38'
First exhibited: Abstract Paintings
by 9 British Artists, Lefevre
Gallery, March 1939 (41)
David Hughes

Painted in London before Evans's
move to South Africa in May. In a
typescript written in early 1938 he
described the message that the artist
should give in a period that he saw
then as being immediately before a
war. He should present 'the aggressive instinct for power and destruction' so that we should know humanity as it is. He exampled Picasso's
'Guernica', which he had seen in
Paris the summer before, and his own
paintings 'Disturbance in the East',
painted on the outbreak of the
Manchuquo Affair, and another
called 'Distressed Area', referring to
Spain.

'Distressed Area' was reproduced in
the Natal Technical College magazine
(*The Common Room*, July 1938) with a
text by the artist. He details each part
as if in a narrative, and refers to
archetypes in a way comparable to
the titles of earlier paintings with a
Freudian use of myth. The exaggera-

tion of his description, more extreme than in his other writings of the time, follows Wyndham Lewis's style in writing, and he does not here refer again to the Spanish Civil War:

'An old vulture hovers over the stage and there are flecks of blood issuing from the disintegrating pustules on his bald head. He is the Carrion King. Below him groups of woodpeckers attack the ice-smooth sides of pyramids. The sky burns like a furnace, and in the background the white-hot embers of a dying cactus arrange themselves like a dying Roman gladiator wrapped in the mandibles of a giant crustacean. On the left in a gesture of supplication a ferocious Oedipus turns to the implac-able beast of prey. On the right, with a cynical parody of Lot and his wife, a mining family, in attitudes of in-credible depravity, are petrified like remote fossils of lapis and emerald. At their feet are fetishes that fill us with lust and longing. They litter the floor of the stage and beckon with a sinister compulsion' (quoted in *The Daily News*, Durban, 15 August 1938).

10 **Polynesian Fantasy** September
1938
Tempera on panel, $7\frac{3}{4} \times 9\frac{3}{4}$
(19.5 × 24.5)
Inscribed on reverse 'Polynesian
Fantasy – September 20 1938'
Margerie Evans

In South Africa Evans painted conventional portraits and landscapes as well as still lifes and imaginative compositions. This small 'Fantasy' is an extension of his still lifes of African plants and fruits.

11 **Untitled Drawing** December
1938
Pencil and white chalk on brown
paper, $12\frac{1}{2} \times 14\frac{1}{2}$ (32 × 37)
Inscribed lower left
'Evans / December 30 1938'
Margerie Evans

This is a finished composition, but a painting was not made from it until after the war, in 1949.

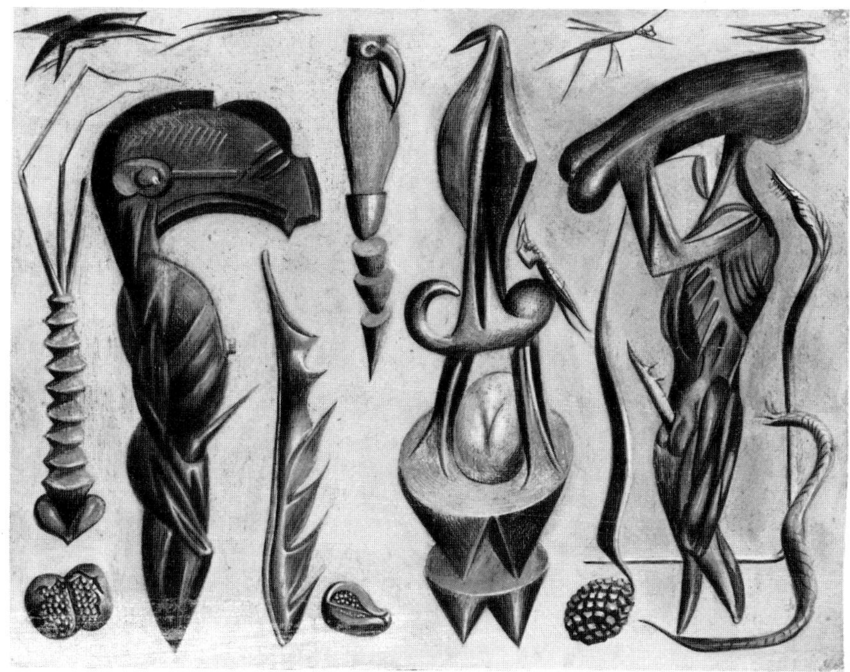

10

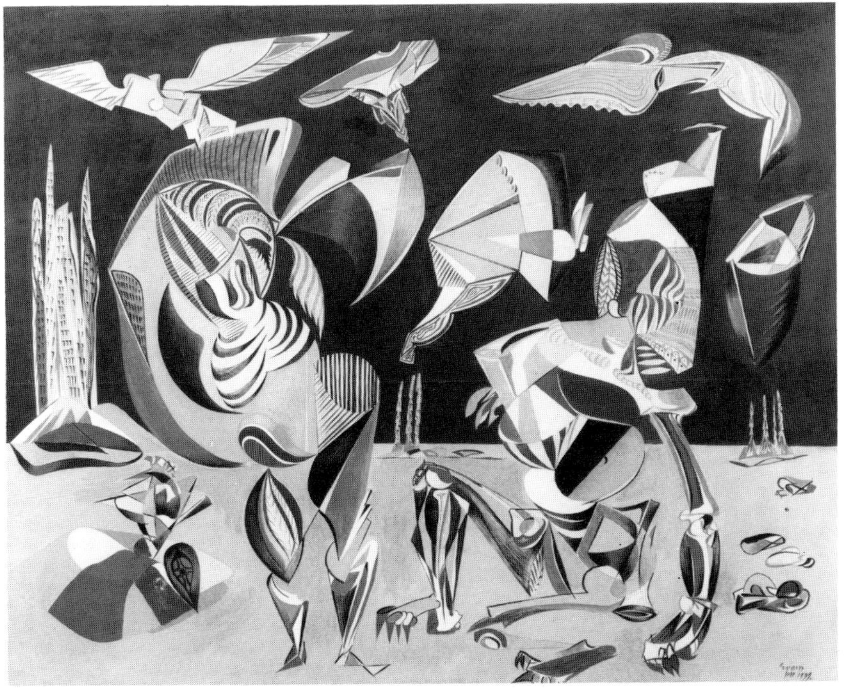

12

African exhibitions, he published a broadsheet of poems in the manner of a manifesto, and one of these links the subject of this painting to a town such as Johannesburg:

'Cities grow precariously, like gigantic cacti. They feed on gold, The cities grow enormous. The city is inorganic and soulless, it is a Tyrannopolis'.

12   Tyrannopolis (The Protestors)
July 1939
Tempera on canvas, 30 × 36
(76 × 91.5)
Inscribed lower right
'Evans July 1939'
First exhibited: Merlyn Evans,
Durban Art Gallery, July 1939
Margerie Evans

Described by the artist, when again exhibited in Durban in April 1940: 'Tyrannopolis is a satire on political economy . . . The beginnings of megalopolitan exodus . . . cessation of productive work in the arts and sciences' (*Natal Daily News*, 3 April 1940). Also, for one of the South

13   Tragic Group (Victims of Demolition) 1939–40
Tempera on panel, 30 × 36
(76 × 91.5)
Inscribed lower left,
'Evans 5th May 1940'
First exhibited: Contemporary South African Paintings, Drawings and Sculpture, Tate Gallery, September 1948 (31, listed in error as 'Victims of Demolition in Tinland, South Africa')
Newport Museum and Art Gallery, Gwent

The subject was etched by the artist in 1949–50, after his return to London. It refers to people displaced by the Russian invasion of Finland in 1939–40. It is the first of the series of war paintings of 1940, and is clear in drawing and much less complicated in imagery than the preceding paintings.

14   The Chess Players 1940
Oil on canvas, 40 × 40
(101.5 × 101.5)
Inscribed 'M.O. Evans / 1940' on book at lower right
First exhibited: Merlyn Evans, The

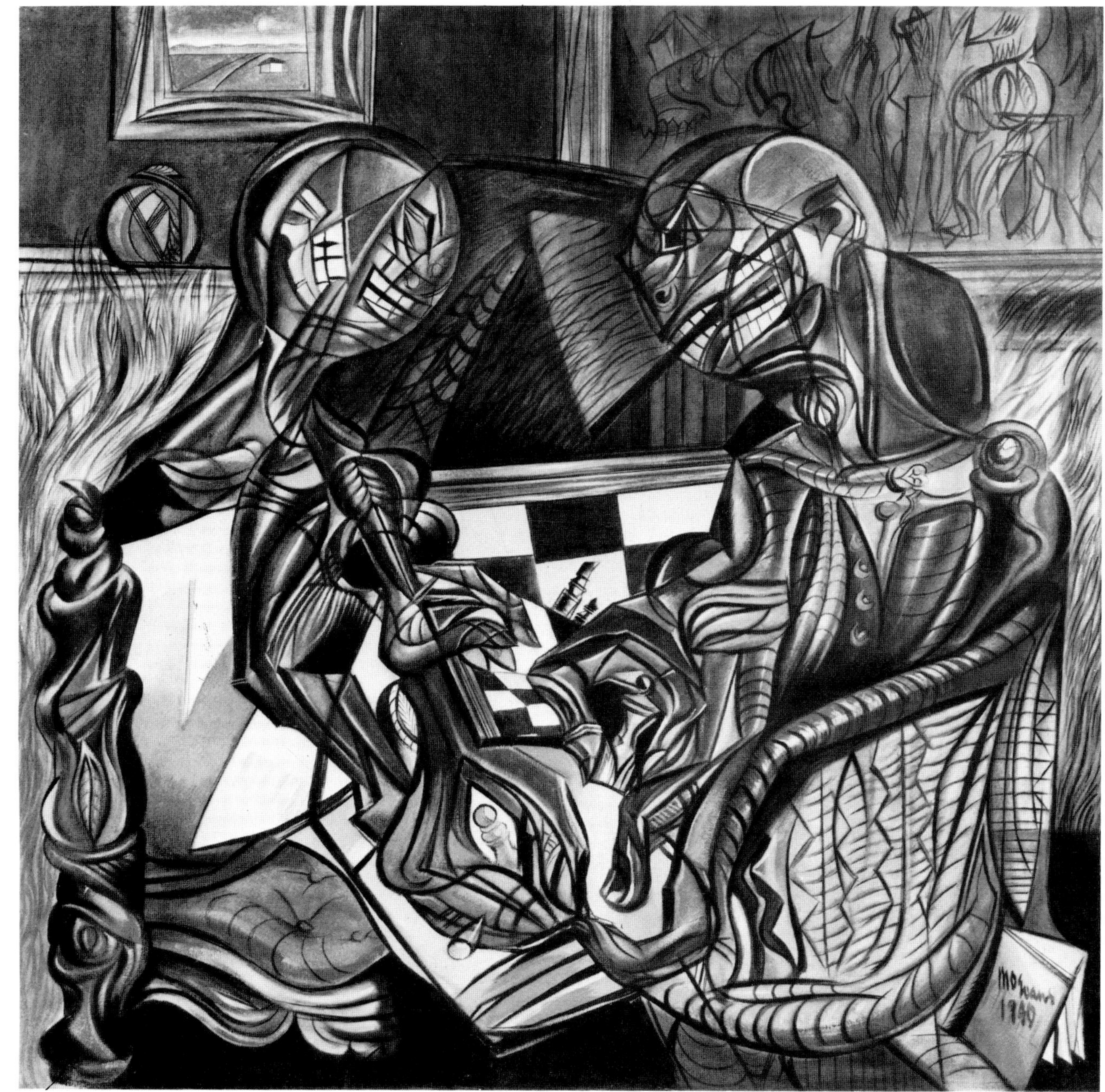

14

Leicester Galleries, February
1949 (19)
Eldred Evans

Printed as an etching and aquatint in
1949–51.
The subject is the non-aggression pact
between Germany and Russia signed
in August 1939. The war followed
shortly after this, and as a major
change of policies for both countries
the pact was immediately seen as a
licence for each to attack its neigh-
bours.

Two finished preparatory drawings
exist (a third one is for the print)
which is unusual, and may indicate
the novelty of such a direct political
subject. In both of these drawings,
and also faintly in the painting, the
name HEGEL is written on the book at
the right, presumably with reference
to the philosopher's acceptance of war
as a policy of vigorous nations. In one
of these drawings a name written at
the left, only faintly visible, is probably BERNSTEIN, referring to Eduard
Bernstein's advocacy of a negotiated
solution to Germany's territorial
claims. The paintings on the wall, a
conventional landscape and a composition like one of Evans's own, may
make the same point as some of his
pre-war writing, that the artist should
not provide an escape into prettiness,
but show to man his own aggressive
nature, now anyway demonstrated
by the war. The implication of the
subject is that the Nazis and Communists, while opposing each other,
will be prepared to sacrifice like pawns
the smaller countries of Europe.

15

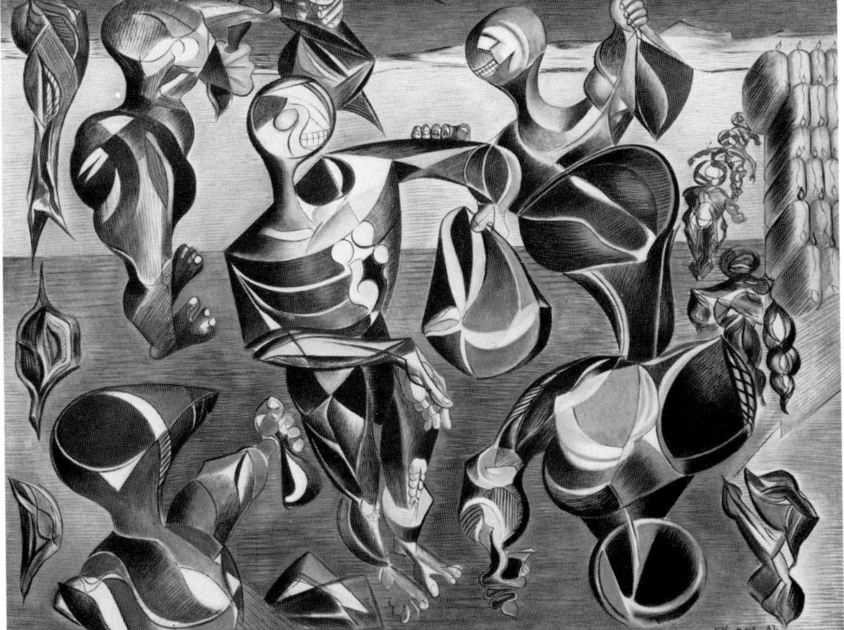

15 The Looters May 1940
Oil on canvas, 40 × 50
(101.5 × 127)
Inscribed lower right 'M.O. Evans
40' and on reverse 'M.O. Evans
May 1940'
First exhibited: Three Modern
Painters, Cecil Higgins Museum,
Bedford, March–April 1955 (10)
Eldred Evans

Listed by the artist as 'The Looters –
Abyssinia', the subject is the Italian
occupation of Abyssinia from 1936.

16 The Puppet Government
1940
Oil on canvas, 67 × 48
(170 × 122)
Inscribed lower left 'Evans 1940'
First exhibited: Merlyn Evans,
Marlborough Fine Art, March
1968 (10)
M.O. Evans Estate

There is no text by the artist explain-
ing this, but the subject is probably
the Quisling government of Norway,
set up by the Germans after their
capture of the country – by the use of
paratroops – in April 1940.

***17 The Conflict (No. 1)**
August – October 1940
Oil on canvas, 40 × 50
(101.5 × 127)
Inscribed lower left 'M. Evans
1940' and on stretcher 'The
Conflict. Aug – Sep – Oct 1940'
First exhibited: Paintings and
Drawings by Merlyn Evans, The
Midland Group, Nottingham, July
1952 (18)
M.O. Evans Estate

The earlier war subjects refer to particular incidents but this, like the subsequent pictures, is based only on the
general idea of conflict.

18 The Mark of the Beast November
1940
Oil on canvas, 36 × 28
(91.5 × 71)
Inscribed on stretcher 'The Mark
of the Beast. 23 Nov 1940'
First exhibited: Merlyn Evans,

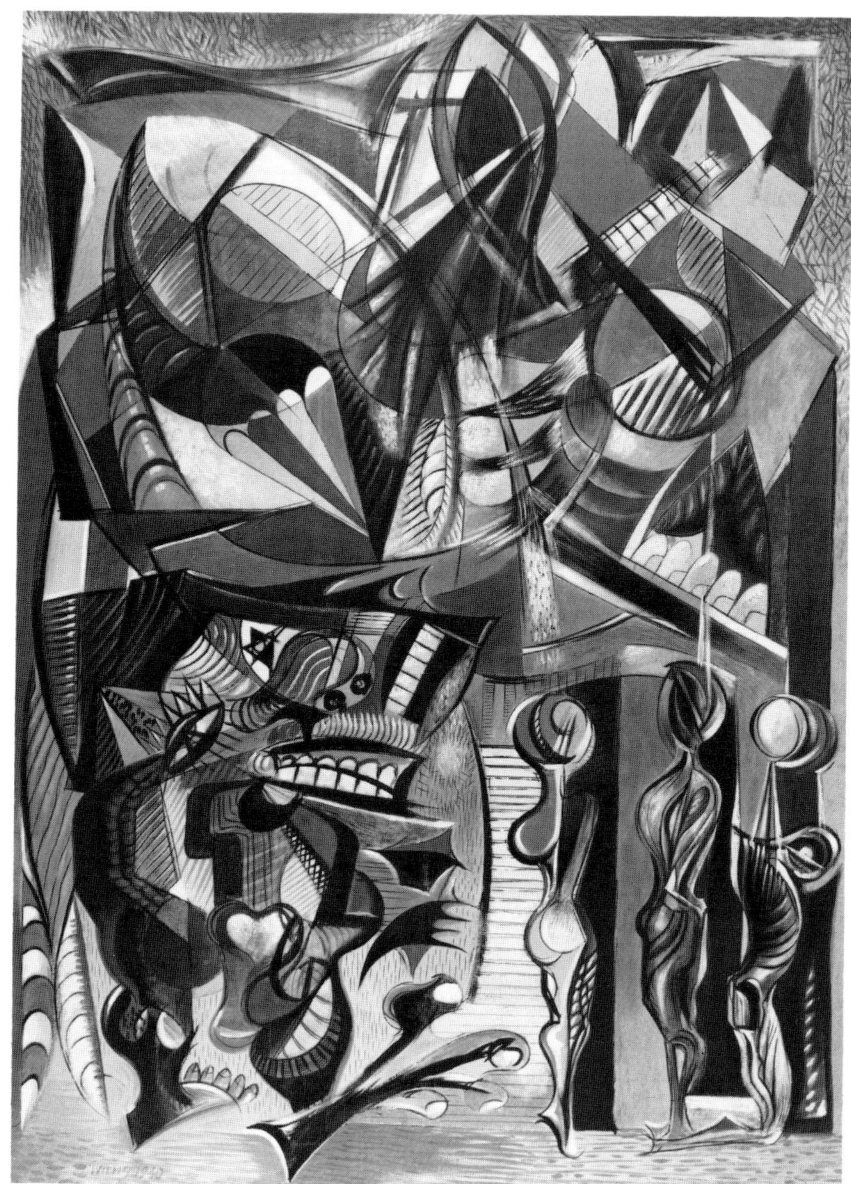

16

New Art Centre, October –
November 1976 (D)
Tate Gallery

Probably a reference to Hitler, and
later listed by the artist as 'The Beast
of Belsen', although he could not have
known of the concentration camp at
the time of the painting.

19   The Entombment   September
1942
Oil on canvas, 40 × 50
(101.5 × 127)
Inscribed '11th Sept 1942 Burial'
and 'The Entombment' on reverse
First exhibited: Merlyn Evans, The
Leicester Galleries, February
1949 (11)
M.O. Evans Estate

The first painting made after Evans
had joined the South African army.
The subject is not the entombment of
Christ, but was put together from a
number of separate private incidents,
and is described in 'Background'
(p.24). At the Leicester Galleries in
1949 it was the highest priced of his
exhibits.

20   Nocturnal Fantasy   1942
Oil on canvas, 40 × 31
(101.5 × 78.5)
Inscribed lower left 'Evans 42'
First exhibited: Merlyn Evans, The
Leicester Galleries, February
1949 (10)
Margerie Evans

Painted during several periods of
leave from army training. This is one
of the most fragmented of the wartime
paintings, and was first worked out in
writing. The subject is described in
'Background' (p.24).

21   Portrait of an Old Soldier   June
1943
Pencil on paper, 22 × 15
(56 × 38)
Inscribed lower left 'Portrait of an
Old Soldier – Spitzkop' and lower
right 'Evans 43' and on jacket
'6/6/43'
First exhibited: Merlyn Evans,
Whitechapel Art Gallery,
October – November 1956 (96)
Margerie Evans

Evans continued while in the army to
make pencil portraits, as he had done
earlier in South Africa, where a considerable number were commissioned
in Durban.

22   Nocturnal Drama   September
1944
Oil on canvas, $27\frac{1}{4} \times 31\frac{1}{2}$
(70 × 80)
Inscribed lower right 'Evans
20/9/44'
First exhibited: 'Annual art show,
Johannesburg' ('Background',
p.25).
Arts Council of Great Britain

One of two paintings made at Tobruk,
and, like no.20, the subject was first
planned in writing.

23   The Drinkers   1944 – 5
Oil on canvas, 26 × 22 (66 × 56)
Inscribed lower left 'Evans
4/10/45' and on stretcher 'The
Drinkers, oil. 1944 Forli Italy'
First exhibited: Merlyn Evans, The
Leicester Galleries, February
1949 (23)
Eldred Evans

Evans moved from North Africa to
Italy with the Eighth Army in 1944,

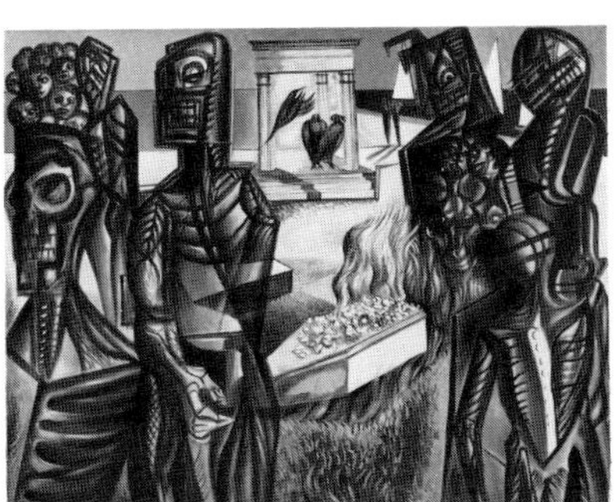

19

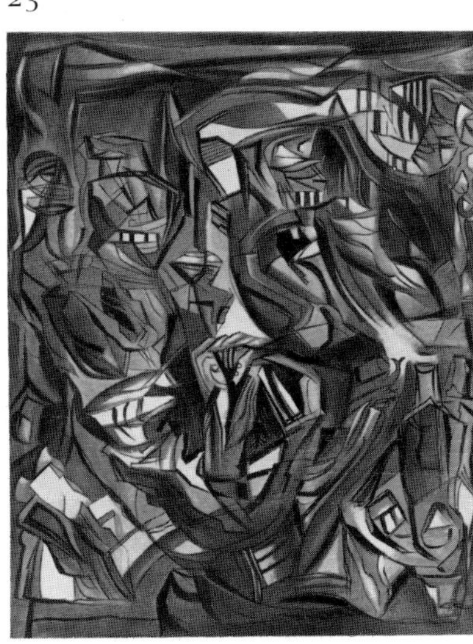

23

and he explains in 'Background' how he was able to paint while resting during the day after night operations. This painting is a repetition, made by him soon after the original had been lost.

24 Paesaggio Tragico April 1945

Oil on canvas, 39 × 47
(99 × 119.5)
Inscribed lower left 'Evans
13/4/45 RAVENNA'
First exhibited: Merlyn Evans, The
Midland Group, Nottingham, July
1952 (1)
New Art Centre

Unusual amongst the war paintings because it is a landscape, the subject is however, as the title suggests, the destruction of the town of Ravenna. Old photographs of the damaged buildings show that the right hand part of the painting is recognisable as a long shed with skylights beside a railway track, and is portrayed accurately. Evans wrote a poem of the same title.

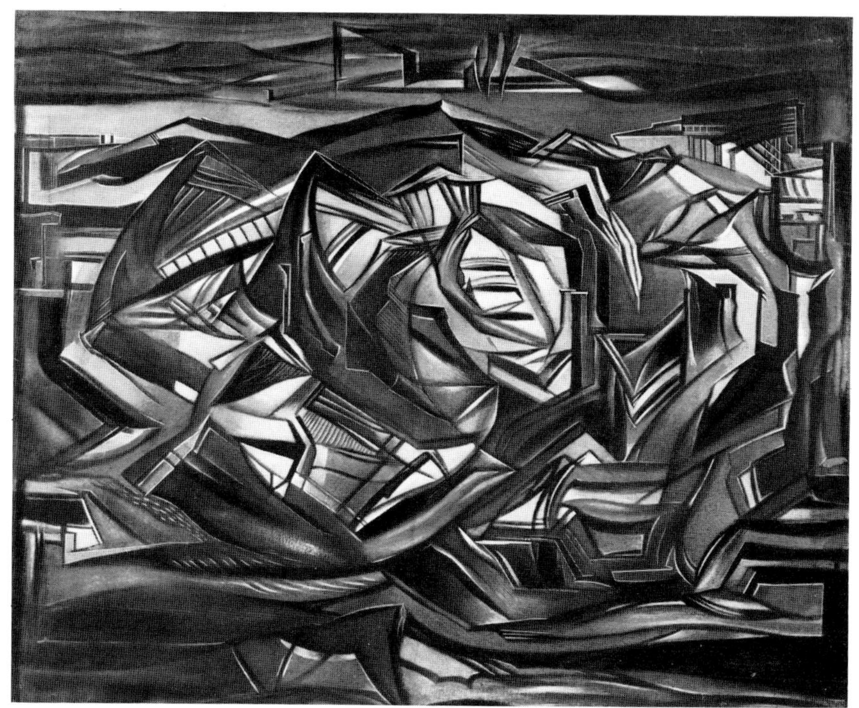

24

25 Giorgio de Chirico July 1945

Pencil on paper, 19½ × 13
(49.5 × 33)
Inscribed lower right, 'Giorgio de
Chirico 25 July at Rome' and
lower left 'Evans '45'
First exhibited: Merlyn Evans,
Watercolours and Drawings, The
Leicester Galleries, February
1952 (7)
Margerie Evans

Evans sought out de Chirico in Rome at the end of the war, since he had for a long time admired his work. The visit is described in 'Background' (p.27).

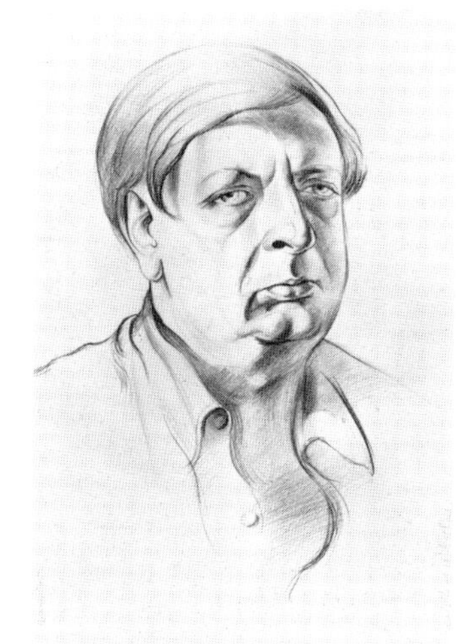

25

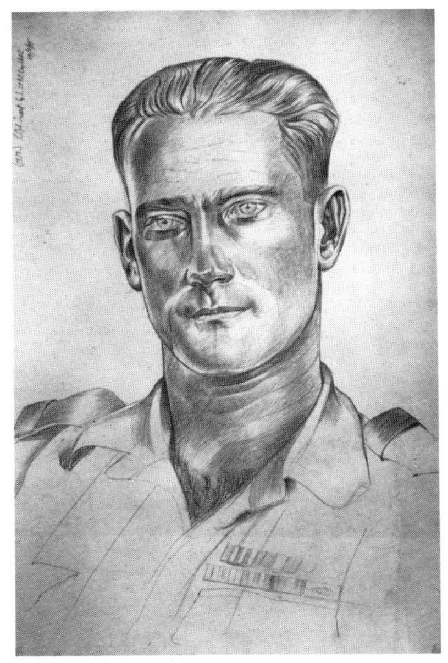

26

26 Lance-Corporal Swart August
1945
Pencil on paper, 20¼ × 14
(51 × 34.5)
Inscribed '(MM) L. Cpl. Swart G.J.
25 R.C. Coy SAEC 24/8/45'
*Trustees of the Imperial War
Museum*

While he was in Rome Evans was
asked to portray South African hol-
ders of the Military Cross and Military
Medal. A group of these drawings
were acquired recently by the
Imperial War Museum.

***27 The Crucifixion** 1945
Oil on canvas, 50 × 29
(127 × 73.5)
Inscribed on label on reverse
'The Crucifixion 1945'
M.O. Evans Estate

The first version of this crucifixion
was painted near Venice in the early
summer of 1945, and was shown in
the Tate Gallery's exhibition of South
African paintings in 1948–9. It now
belongs to Nottingham Castle Art
Gallery. The painting exhibited here
seems to be a second version painted
shortly later, and in it the shapes and
outlines are more precise but are less
easy to read and more abstract. Many
of the details differ, and in the Nottingham version it is easier to see that this
strange Crucifixion includes a foreground of insects. Merlyn Evans did
hold Christian beliefs but did not paint
other religious subjects, apart from
student work. It is possible that this
Crucifixion, like the Entombment of
1942 (no.19), is as much personal
and contemporary as Biblical.

28

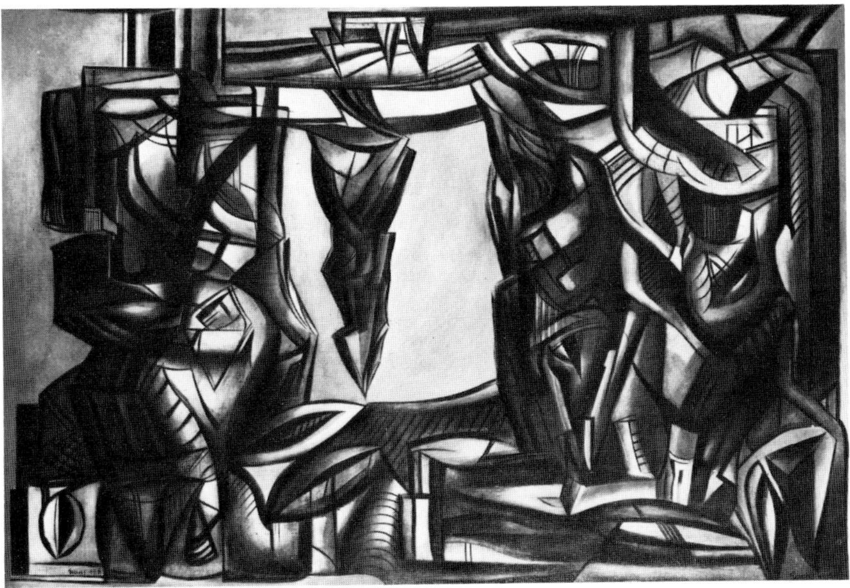

28 The Execution 1945–6
Oil on canvas, 33 × 47
(84 × 119.5)
Inscribed lower left 'Evans 45–6'
and lower right 'Evans 45'
First exhibited: Merlyn Evans, The
Leicester Galleries, February
1949 (1)
*Trustees of the Imperial War
Museum*

Printed as an etching and aquatint in
1946–8, and one of the first subjects
painted after Merlyn Evans's return to
London and demobilisation in 1945.
Margerie Evans identifies the subject
as the death of Mussolini, although
the figures cannot be specified. The
abstract figure at the left, whether
victim or spectator, became a particular preoccupation and reappears
in 'The Stranger' (1946, no.20), 'The
Prisoner' (1947, no.31) and 'The
Trial' (1949).

29 The Stranger 1946
Oil on canvas over board,
$13\frac{1}{2} \times 9\frac{1}{4}$ (34 × 23.5)
Inscribed lower left 'Evans 46'
Andrew Murray

Printed as an engraving and aquatint
the same size and in the same year.

30 The Refugees December 1946
Oil on canvas, 42 × 32
(106.5 × 81.5)
Inscribed lower left 'Evans 46'
and lower right 'DECEMBER 46'
First exhibited: Artists of Fame
and Promise, II, The Leicester
Galleries, August 1947 (134)
National Museum of Wales

Listed by the artist as 'Refugees at
Spezia'.

31 The Prisoner August 1947
Oil on canvas, 24 × 20 (61 × 51)
Inscribed lower right 'Evans 47'
and on reverse 'begun 21st
August'
First exhibited: Merlyn Evans, The
Leicester Galleries, February
1949 (12)
Morris Kestelman

Printed as a colour aquatint in 1953.
The figure appears as the central
'prisoner' in the large painting of
1949 'The Trial' 36 × 60
(91.5 × 152.5), National Gallery of
New South Wales, Adelaide. The trial
is not a specific event, although influenced by the Nuremberg trials of
1945–7.

32 Self Portrait 1952
Pencil on paper, $20\frac{1}{2} \times 15$
(52 × 38)
Inscribed on lapel 'Evans 52.'
Tate Gallery Archive

Drawn for *Art News and Review*,
which published a series of reviews on
artists' work with self portraits, for
their issue of 23 February 1952.

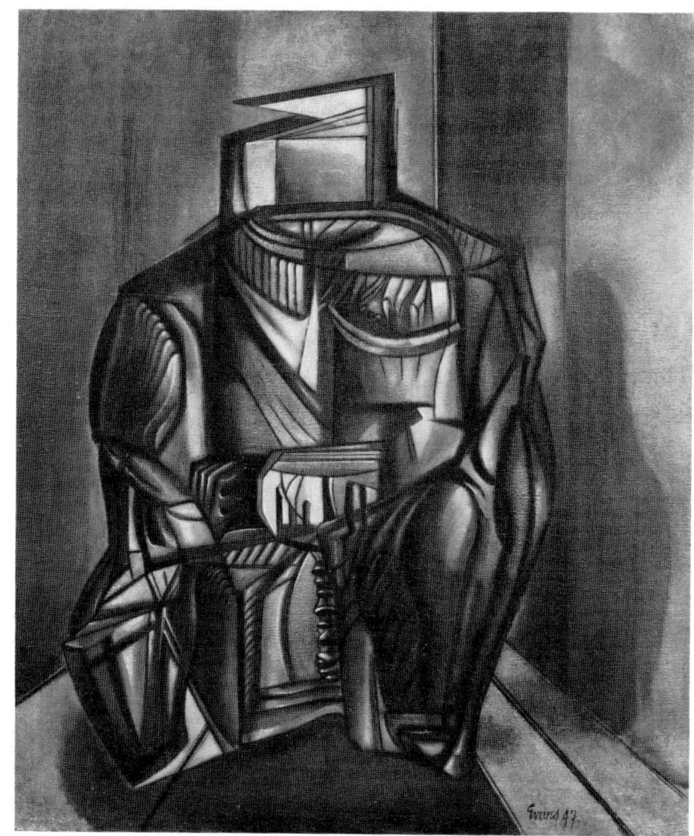

31

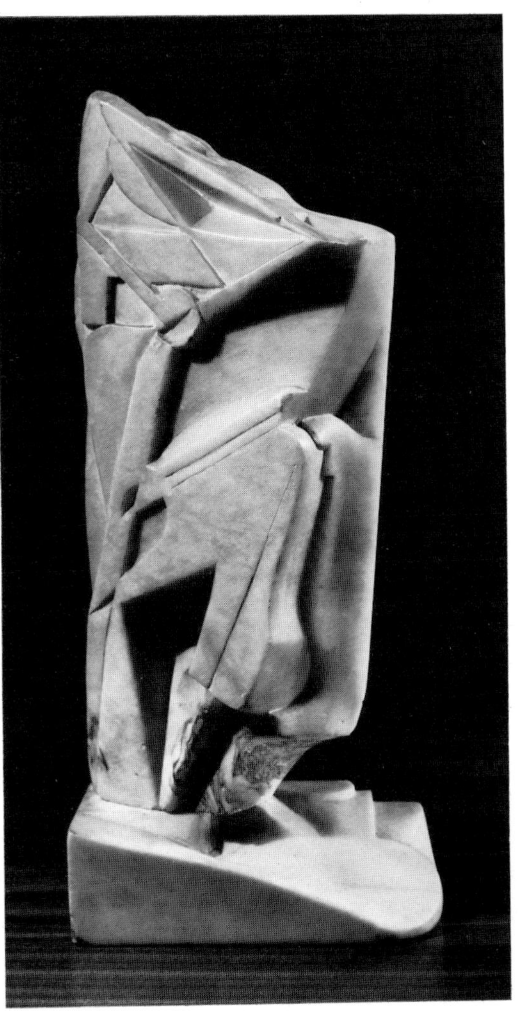

33

33 Carving *c.1932–3*
Red veined alabaster,
22¾ (58) high
Margerie Evans

34 Carving *c.1932–3*
Marble, 23½ (59.5) high, without
base
Margerie Evans

35 Carving *c.1932–3*
Red veined alabaster,
13 (33) high
Exhibited: Merlyn Evans, The
Leicester Galleries, February
1949 (32)
Margerie Evans

It was probably these carvings that
were made at his home while Evans
was a student at the Royal College, 'in
the backyard of my lodgings under
the tuition of Mr Cobbold, a stone
mason' ('Background', p.23). As in
the case of some of the earliest abstract drawings, these show his interest in sculpture by Lawrence
Atkinson, but are otherwise remark-
ably unlike contemporary sculpture.
Evans made small reliefs and carvings
throughout his career, but this interest was always secondary, except
for the sixty foot screen he made for
Tower Hamlets Comprehensive
School in 1964.

Merlyn Evans, 1910–1973

BIOGRAPHY TO 1950

1910

13 March, born in Llandaff, Cardiff. Father an analytical chemist, mother formerly a nurse. In spite of living there for so short a time, Evans always referred to himself as Welsh

1913

Family moved to Rutherglen, Glasgow.
Pupil at Rutherglen Academy; Allen Glen's School, Glasgow. Private lessons in painting from the brothers John and Charles Houston

1927–31

Glasgow School of Art.
First abstract work by Evans is dated 1930, but his earlier interest in Renaissance painting continued, and he used a tempera technique and made a finished copy of a Crivelli Madonna

1930 and 1931

Exhibited at Royal Scottish Academy

1931

Awarded Haldane Travelling Scholarship from Glasgow School of Art (£50) and visited Berlin, Copenhagen (staying with his relation, the academic painter Mathias Koedt) and Paris. He admired work by Feininger, Gris, Klee and Kandinsky seen on exhibition

1932

Entered competition for scholarship of British School at Rome, and exhibited large mural painting 'Christ driving the money-changers out of the Temple', which was 'highly commended'

1932–4

Royal College of Art, entering with a scholarship. Evans did not respond to the teaching, which did not encourage abstract art. Took private lessons in carving, and made a series of large abstract drawings. Influenced by the drawings and sculpture of Lawrence Atkinson (1873–1931), illustrated in a book by Horace Shipp 'The New Art' (1922)

1933

Again entered Rome Scholarship competition

1934

Married Phyllis Sullivan, fellow painting student at the Royal College, and lived in Streatham. This marriage was dissolved during the war. First painting with political subject, 'The Suppliants'. Frequent visits to Paris during 1930s, on one occasion visiting the studios of Mondrian, Ernst, Kandinsky and Hayter

1934–6

Art Master at Wilson's Grammar School, Camberwell

1936

Reviewed David Gascoyne's 'A short survey of surrealism' (1935).
June, 'International Surrealist Exhibition', New Burlington Galleries. Evans showed three paintings ('The Conquest of Time', 1934; 'Mother and Son', 1935; 'Count Cenci', 1936), two drawings and two collages.
He was not a leading member of the group and did not consider himself a surrealist. His closest artist friends were then Charles Howard, the American-born abstract painter, and F.E. McWilliam

1936–8

Taught at Riemann's School, Victoria, a school of design directed by Austin Cooper, where Moholy-Nagy and Charles Howard were also teaching

1937

April, exhibited at Artists' International Association, 41 Grosvenor Square, two paintings ('The Encounter Between Laius and Electra' and 'Freud Transferring the Burden of his Guilt to Oedipus')
October, exhibited one work, 'The

Hermaphrodite', at the London
Group.
November, exhibited two collages in
'Surrealist Objects & Poems', London
Gallery (including 'Les Fleurs du
Mal').
December, sees exhibition of
Wyndham Lewis at the Leicester
Galleries

1938

January, assisted at M.A.R.S. architectural exhibition, New Burlington
Galleries.
May, moved to Durban, South Africa,
as lecturer in art at Natal Technical
College

1939

March, exhibited in 'Abstract Paintings by 9 British Artists' at Lefevre
Gallery (seven works, lent from store
as Evans was in South Africa).
July, first one-man exhibition, at
Durban Art Gallery. Painted large
mural at Natal Technical College
(since destroyed)

1940

Proposed, unsuccessfully, the organisation of official South African war
artists. Continued to paint portraits
and landscapes as well as abstract
works, and made sculpture

1940–1

Numerous paintings of war subjects

1942

Enlisted in a Signals company in the
South African army, and later transferred to Engineers. Was able to paint
during training and on leave

1943–5

Moved with Eighth Army to North
Africa and Italy

1945

August, transferred to War Records in
Rome, and made portrait drawings of
South African soldiers.
Met and drew de Chirico
Returned to London and discovered
that many of his pre-war paintings
had been destroyed.

1946

Took refresher course at the Central
School, studying etching and aquatint
under W.P. Robins. Began series of
large aquatints. Lived at 21 Mecklenberg Square

1947

May, exhibited one painting ('Woman
in Interior') at London Group

1948

September, 'Exhibition of Contemporary South African Paintings, Drawings and Sculpture', Tate Gallery
(4 paintings)

1949

February, 'Imaginative Paintings by
Merlyn Evans', The Leicester
Galleries, preface by Roy Campbell
(29 paintings and 3 sculptures).
Wyndham Lewis, who had recently
met Evans for the first time, recommended the exhibition by letter to
James Thrall Soby

1950

Married the pianist Margerie Few,
whose sister Elsie was married to
Claude Rogers

Selected Exhibitions

ONE MAN

1939 July
Durban Art Gallery, South Africa
(no catalogue).

1949 February
Imaginative Paintings by Merlyn Evans,
The Leicester Galleries. Preface by Roy
Campbell.

1952 February
*Watercolours and Drawings by Merlyn
Evans*, The Leicester Galleries.

1953 March
New Paintings, The Leicester Galleries.
Preface by J.P. Hodin.

1955 November
New Paintings, The Leicester Galleries.

1956 October – November
Whitechapel Art Gallery. Preface by
Bryan Robertson, notes by the artist.
Abstract Painting and Merlyn Evans
by R.H. Wilenski.

1958 February – March
Vertical Suite in Black, St. George's
Gallery Prints.

1958 November
New Paintings, The Leicester Galleries.

1963 October
Paintings, reliefs and drawings.
McRoberts and Tunnard Ltd. Preface
by the artist.

1967 February – March
Exchange artist in residence from the
Royal College of Art, Art Institute of
Chicago.

1968 March
Merlyn Evans, Events and Abstractions,
Marlborough New London Gallery.
Preface by the artist.

1972 November – December
New Art Centre.

1972–3 November – February
The Graphic Work of Merlyn Evans,
Victoria and Albert Museum. Intro-
duction by Robert Erskine, The ab-
stract images of Merlyn Evans by
Bryan Robertson.

1974 June – August
Merlyn Evans 1910–1973, National
Museum of Wales, Cardiff, travelling
to Glasgow Museum and Art Gallery,
August–September 1974.
Introduction by Frederick Laws.

1974 July – September
Tribute to Merlyn Evans, 1910–1973,
Bradford Art Gallery.

1975 February – March
Ten paintings, 1930–1955, New Art
Centre.

1976 June – July
*Merlyn Evans, an exhibition of draw-
ings: portraits, nudes and metamorphic
figures.* Scottish National Gallery of
Modern Arts, Edinburgh, travelling to
New Art Centre, October – November
1976.

1981 February
Seven Paintings 1965–1968, New Art
Centre.

1983 June
Drawings from the 1930s, New Art
Centre.

1984 April – May
Merlyn Evans: etchings 1930–73,
Newport Museum and Art Gallery.

List of Lenders

GROUP EXHIBITIONS

1936 June
International Surrealist Exhibition, New Burlington Galleries.

1939 March
Abstract Paintings by 9 British Artists, Lefevre Gallery.

1948–9 September–January
Exhibition of Contemporary South African Paintings, Drawings and Sculpture, Tate Gallery.

1950 January–February
New Paintings by Merlyn Evans, Cecil Collins, Francis Rose, The Heffer Gallery, Cambridge.

1953–4 December–February
II Bienal, Sao Paulo.

1955 March–April
Three Modern Painters, Cecil Higgins Museum, Bedford (with William Gear and Ceri Richards).

1962 October–November
British Art and the Modern Movement 1930–40, National Museum of Wales, Cardiff.

1965 March–April
Art in Britain 1930–40, Centred around Axis, Circle, Unit One. Marlborough Fine Art Ltd and Marlborough New London Gallery.

Arts Council of Great Britain 22
Eldred Evans 14, 15, 23
Margerie Evans 1, 3, 4, 7, 8, 10, 11, 12, 20, 21, 25, 33, 34, 35
M.O. Evans Estate 16, 17, 19, 27
David Hughes 9
Trustees of the Imperial War Museum 26, 28
Morris Kestelman 31
Andrew Murray 29
National Museum of Wales 2, 30
New Art Centre 24
Newport Museum and Art Gallery 13
Private Collection 6
Tate Gallery 5, 18, 32